"Men wear a suit because it's the gear of the gentleman the world over."

Hardy Amies, *The Englishman's Suit*

SHARP
SUITS

Eric Musgrave

Foreword by Richard James

PAVILION

CONTENTS

Cover: (Front) From 1966, this high-fastening six-button suit by Ted Lapidus, worn with all the right accessories for a gentleman, displays the passion of Paris. (Back) Cary Grant radiates class in a 1940s double-breasted suit.

Endpapers: Scenes from the Brioni hand-tailoring workshop in Penne, Italy.

Page 2: Steve McQueen reaches the pinnacle of style in *The Thomas Crown Affair* in 1968. His fabulous suits for the movie were styled by London showbiz tailor Douglas Hayward. Usually a casual dresser, McQueen wore the suits for several weeks before filming began to get used to the feel of fine tailoring.

Left: It takes a lot of height and a lot of personal style to carry off an eight-button double-breasted suit, no matter how well cut. Spanish nobleman Don Jaime de Mesia Figueroa shows us how it's done while striking a pose next to his Matra sports car in about 1967. The photographer was Patrick, Lord Lichfield.

Foreword

Like most men of my age, my attitude to suits has changed over the years and I have all sorts of memories of the ones I've owned. I remember my father, an oil salesman in the West Country of England, always wore a dark suit from Burton's. All the suits were dark in those days. Around 1970, when I was about seventeen, I got my first suit, a hand-me-down from my Uncle Jack, who was an interior designer in London, which was a very exotic job. It was a pale grey suit from Daks and, living in Bristol, I'd never seen a pale grey suit before.

When I was at Brighton Art College in the 1970s, I might wear a suit to attend a wedding, but like everyone else, I was more likely to be in loon pants and a scoop-neck T-shirt. After college I wanted to be a fashion photographer, so, to get into the fashion business, I started working in the menswear department of Browns, the hugely influential boutique on London's South Molton Street. Suddenly I was travelling the world as a buyer and surrounded by fabulous clothes. I remember in 1982 being given a wonderful three-piece, reddish brown suit in satin by the brilliant Italian designer Walter Albini. It was great, but I never wore it.

I went to the early Armani and Versace menswear catwalk shows in the 1980s. Armani was fantastic. Even though we didn't realise it at the time, he changed the face of men's fashion for ever. After Armani, rather than fathers introducing their sons to their tailors in Savile Row, the sons were introducing their fathers to Armani.

I wore Armani for years, along with other Italian labels such as Basile and Cerruti, and then the Japanese label Comme des Garçons.

I was never into sportswear fashion or streetwear. When I started my own business in the late 1980s with my business partner Sean Dixon, we began with a belief in classic clothes. We took a tiny shop at 37a Savile Row in 1992, at a time when big international fashion labels like Gucci and Yohji Yamamoto were dominant. But our approach was to be different, to be English and to be a little eccentric. Men who were wearing our clothes, bespoke or ready-made, were noticed and complimented. We started a trend in which men wore clothes because they fitted well and looked good, not because of the label in the jacket.

We soon earned a reputation for our suits because we thought about them and what they should do. A good suit makes you look better, move better and feel better. We became recognised for making classic suits that were flattering. Our success enabled us to move to our large shop on Savile Row in 1994 and add our bespoke shop across the road on Clifford Street in 2000. We are now really well-known for our tailoring, and, as a designer, I see my suits always evolving. Classic doesn't stay classic very long.

As *Sharp Suits* illustrates so wonderfully, suits as we know them today have continuously evolved for well over a hundred years. I really enjoyed seeing so many great, stylish photographs of suits in the book, many of which I hadn't seen before. It is interesting to note how many of the vintage suits look modern. I also learned a lot about the history of suits that I didn't know. I'm sure that anyone who enjoys suits will enjoy *Sharp Suits*. This is a lovely book.

Richard James
Savile Row, London, 2009

Introduction

If clothes maketh the man, then the most masculine outfit of them all is the suit. Oh, how well a man can express himself – and impress others – with his suit! *Sharp Suits* is a celebration of a century or so of marvellous tailoring and the men (and occasionally women) who produced it and wore it.

About three metres of fabric, some clever unseen internal shaping elements, lining, buttons and several metres of thread are the simple raw materials that are required to produce the jacket-and-trouser combination (enhanced, in its most sublime form, by a waistcoat) that will be seen wherever men gather, from boardrooms to bawdy bars.

The suit is versatile. When a man wants to look anonymous, he can wear a suit. When he wants to be noticed by his peers or a prospective mate, he can wear a different suit. On every continent, the sober suit is the chosen dress code of presidents and diplomats, business leaders and lawmakers. At its most classic, the suit embodies respectability. Yet it also provides effective camouflage. Not everyone who puts on the uniform of a gentleman *is* a gentleman. Some of the most notorious villains on the planet have been renowned for the quality of their tailoring.

As the bedrock of a stylish man's appearance, a suit defines what his shirt and tie, even his shoes, will look like. Despite the greater acceptance of casualwear as everyday apparel, the suit remains the universal choice of those who want to dress for success. It is a masculine status symbol, especially in the true bespoke version, hand-tailored by artisans using methods that have changed little in a hundred years. Most men today buy ready-made, 'off-the-peg' suits and the excellence of the best of these has never been higher, the result of more than a century of refinements in production methods and fabric quality.

So many subtle nuances make the suit a quite amazing piece of three-dimensional design and engineering. How does the shoulder of the jacket fit? How deep is the armhole? How much 'fullness' is there in the chest? Is the waist defined? Single-breasted or double-breasted? How many buttons? Wide lapels or narrow lapels? Peaked lapels or notched lapels? Flapped pockets or patch pockets or jetted pockets? Flat-fronted trousers or pleated trousers? Wide leg or narrow leg? Turn-ups or no turn-ups?

The suit offers endless stylistic possibilities before we even start to factor in that most essential ingredient, the fabric itself – fine wool or heavier wool, cotton, linen, silk, mohair, polyester mixes, velvet, corduroy, stretch fabrics, jacquard weaves, 'performance fabrics', stripes, checks ... And so the list goes on. Who now can dare say that the suit is boring?

The chapters in *Sharp Suits* are not an exhaustive history of the suit, but rather eight separate essays on aspects of the outfit and its rich heritage. Retro or modern, bold or discreet, the suit remains the ultimate centrepiece of a stylish man's wardrobe. Movie stars and rock stars, heroes and villains, philanthropists and gangsters – all these men and millions more know that suits will suit them very well.

Eric Musgrave

Right: Careful, you could cut yourself on those lapels. A study in English bespoke tailoring expertise from about 1956. Alas, the creator has not been recorded on the photograph, but he certainly knew how to use a covered button and a jetted pocket.

"*A man should look as if he had bought his clothes with intelligence, put them on with care and then forgotten all about them.*"

Hardy Amies, *An ABC of Men's Fashion*

Above: In Tokyo in June 1966, Paul McCartney samples some local tailoring skills in an idiosyncratic suit with strong naval or frock-coat overtones. A ten-button double-breasted jacket is a rare treat indeed. Compare this one to the white option on page 16.

Left: The British aristocrat at rest: Robin Sinclair, 2nd Viscount Thurso, wears his splendid Aquascutum suit well in about 1985, as he brings a sporting look into the lounge. And with a check that bold, it's no wonder the whippet looks startled.

chapter ONE
Convention or Fashion?

I knew exactly what I wanted my new suit to look like. It was in an ad in *L'Uomo Vogue*, the Italian men's fashion magazine. Double-breasted, peaked lapels, in a light-brown Glen check with a light-blue overcheck. Made by Lubiam of Italy, it carried the Egon von Furstenberg label. Sharp, very sharp, I thought, and not the sort of suit that was readily available to a man of limited means in the UK in the early 1980s.

In 1983 I was deputy editor of *Men's Wear* magazine in London. I had been offered a made-to-measure suit by Burton, the venerable chain founded by Montague Burton in 1904. It had been a pioneer of supplying ready-made suits to the masses and, eighty years on, it was trying to recapture the younger customer (I was about twenty-seven at the time) who was then shopping elsewhere.

I headed off to the Tottenham Court Road branch in Central London for my appointment. The suit-department manager was a gent of about sixty who knew I had been sent with the blessing of Burton's head office. Choosing the cloth was easy. In the bunches – the books containing swatches of fabric – I soon found the check I wanted. The manager then showed me simple line diagrams of the different styles of jacket and trousers that were available for the made-to-measure customer. I told him I knew exactly what I wanted and produced the ad, reluctantly torn from my *L'Uomo Vogue*.

His face dropped and his previously pleasant demeanour changed. 'But you can't have a double-breasted suit in the fabric you've chosen,' he insisted. 'It's a sports-jacket fabric. It has to be single-breasted.'

I was somewhat confused, as I imagined that made-to-measure meant I could have what I wanted. I politely insisted that what I wanted was a double-breasted suit in my chosen check. The manager gave in with little good grace. I can't remember his exact words, but the implication was 'Well, OK, if you want to look ridiculous, you can have what you want.'

My suit duly arrived and, while it was not the best suit I have ever owned, it was pretty good, made me feel great, looked the business and attracted many compliments. But the exchange I experienced back then in the early 1980s represented the battle of the old school of traditional tailoring versus the new(er) school of 'fashion'. It's a theme that has run through menswear for the past fifty years at least.

Central to this conflict is the role of the men's suit. For some, the suit is a classic outfit that must adhere to rigorous rules; to others, the suit is just another platform from which to project a regularly changing fashionable image. The former camp insists that the suit must not deviate far from a proven classic norm; the latter see the suit as a vehicle for considerable interpretation. The cyclical nature of men's fashion, while not as fast-moving as women's, ensures that classics sometimes come back into fashion, albeit with a modern twist, which merely confuses matters further.

The suit – a jacket and trousers of matching cloth, occasionally augmented by a waistcoat – has been a staple of a well-dressed man's wardrobe for well over a hundred years. The suit we recognise today was pretty much formed by around 1860 when it was known formally as the lounge suit, a term still used today on invitations to indicate the dress code for occasions that do not require a black-tie outfit.

Previous page: Hardy Amies in relaxed mood at home in England in 1973. Despite his imperious views on convention, he always urged that the suit should be made relevant to the contemporary times. Note the stylish belt loops.

Right: In bespoke tailoring, the trousers are always fitted first. This is a shot from a *Picture Post* story from 1939 entitled 'Making a Savile Row Suit'.

Above: The Prince of Wales, later Edward VII, favours an early lounge suit in 1864. The essentials of the suit have changed little since then.

Left: The nineteenth-century frock-coat influence is seen outside the influential Hung On You boutique, at 430 Kings Road, Chelsea, in 1966.

Shown above, the photograph taken in 1864 of the Prince of Wales (later Edward VII), his wife Alexandra and their first-born, Prince Albert, encapsulates the early look perfectly. Proving that what goes around, comes around, the soft-shoulder, single-breasted style, with a high fastening revealing relatively little of the shirt at the neck, was a style that enjoyed a revival in the modern mass market as recently as the late 1990s.

Until after the Second World War, polite society in the UK took its fashion lead from the royal family. And, without exaggerating too much, the rest of the world took its lead from what the British wore. For centuries, the social mores and dress codes of the nation had been dictated by the court and then disseminated by the aristocracy, who were, literally, the leaders of men. For the origins of the modern suit, we must look back to the court of Charles II in the late 1660s. By then the restored king was wearing a long jacket of Persian origin, a long waistcoat underneath it, and breeches, a form of trousers that reached the knee.

Under pressure from the financial demands of a difficult naval war with the Dutch, which were compounded by the calamities of the Great Plague of 1665 and the Great Fire of London in September the following year, Charles II decreed in October 1666 that the court should simplify its dress by wearing appropriately sombre three-piece outfits of the same dark fabric.

Although the court did not long remain out of its usual finery – after all, clothes have always been a manifestation of wealth and power – costume historians recognise this period as the starting point for the evolution of the three-piece suit.

One modern connection with Charles II's time is in the way men's jackets fasten: the buttons were sewn on to the right side so that a man could easily unbutton them with his left hand as he used his right hand to draw his sword, which was always worn on the left side.

From the early seventeenth century, the suit developed its modern shape through the adaptation of riding clothes. Unlike their French counterparts, the English aristocracy did not stay long at court. They spent many months on their country estates, where the main leisure activity was hunting on horseback, racing or simply riding. The jacket worn at court was too long to be practical for riding, so it was cut away at the front, with edges that sloped from the centre, and dropped to tails at the back. Sleeves and cuffs were narrowed. By the close of the eighteenth century, this sporting cutaway jacket had become daywear, worn with a waistcoat and knee breeches.

While tightly woven silk was a typical fabric for court clothes, wool cloth was preferred for the great outdoors. According to costume historian Norah Waugh, 'by the end of the eighteenth century, English tailors became the leaders of men's fashions because their long experience of the subtleties of cloth had developed their skill and they gave style and elegance to the practical country coats and so made them acceptable for fashion wear.'[1]

Between 1789 and 1820 the Prince Regent (later George IV) was the first of a series of royals to be an arbiter of fashion and style. The prince was adopted for a time by the great figure of men's fashion, George 'Beau' Brummell, who set new standards of taste. Although he is often wrongly described as a dandy, meaning a flamboyant dresser, Brummell's entire ethos was about decorum and correctness, not extravagance. Costume historian James Laver has argued that Brummell's revolution of simplicity represented a recognition that 'the day of aristocracy was over and that the day of gentility had arrived'.[2]

Another key development from the Beau was that he had his clothes tailored to fit him snugly. Previously the clothes of the aristocracy were badly made and fitted loosely – they were all sewn by hand. 'George Brummell prided himself on the fact that his clothes did not show a single wrinkle and that his breeches fitted him like a second skin,' wrote Laver.[3]

By 1820, however, trousers were becoming more common, although they were rather shapeless, not showing the profile of the leg, and stopping above the ankle.

As a further advancement, the riding coat was adapted to have a front cut straight across. By the nineteenth century this garment, known as a 'tailcoat', was acceptable wear for all dressy occasions, except for events at the royal court. Today it remains with us only in the very formal outfits of orchestra conductors, toastmasters, ballroom dancers and waiters at a few smart, old-fashioned restaurants.

As riding was a popular morning pastime for gentlemen, the old-style jacket with sloping front edges became known as a 'morning coat' and was deemed acceptable on more informal gatherings. It remains with us today, is often seen at Ascot and has enjoyed a recent revival with bridegrooms, usually appearing as a black jacket worn with striped trousers. By the later part of the nineteenth century it was vying for dominance in a gentlemen's wardrobe with the smart frock-coat. Usually double-breasted and fastening high to the neck, the frock-coat clearly had a military heritage. Reaching well below mid-thigh, it was of a similar length to the dress coat and morning coat, but had a less raffish air. Norah Waugh describes it as 'a very worthy and somewhat dull garment, a coat for the well-to-do and professional classes – the hallmark of Victorian respectability'.[4] I think she is being unfair; I regard the frock-coat as being rather stylish, even authoritarian. It, too, enjoys a revival in special-occasion wear these days, but more significantly it is a direct ancestor of the double-breasted suit jacket.

Since the early 1800s, by the unfastening of the top button and turning back the fabric to open the coat, the origins of the modern single-breasted revers or lapels was created. The buttonhole that was on the left lapel is retained for decoration today or, very occasionally, to hold a flower.

By the middle of the nineteenth century, as the middle-class expanded its numbers, flamboyance and colour began to disappear from men's clothes. In the UK, the sober Protestant work ethic began to hold sway in the new world of commerce and trade. In the social mores of the era, which persisted well into the twentieth century, a gentleman had no need or inclination to wear anything that would be noticed as striking. Beau Brummell's gospel held true: 'If John Bull turns round to look after you, you are not well dressed: but either too stiff, too tight or too fashionable.'[5]

As the Victorian era drew to a close, there was increasing use of what was regarded as informal attire – namely, the

This smart D.B. Suit, individually styled, carries the hall-mark of good taste. Tailored to give the fine details and perfection of finish distinguishing clothes of the highest grade. Tailored of quality woollens, including pin-checks, shadow stripes, overplaids, shadow checks, pin-stripes, chalk-stripes, etc., as well as the plain shades of navy blue and brown. For smart and stylish appearance and sound and honest value invest in a Montague Burton Suit to-day

5 guinea value
D.B. SUIT
to-measure for 55/!

Above: The ultimate 'multiple tailor', Montague Burton, The Tailor of Taste, was reckoned to have made suits for one in every five men in the UK in the 1930s. For five guineas (today's £5.25), the ordinary man could dress like a gentleman.

lounge suit – although a frock-coat or morning coat was still *de rigueur* among high society when in London, making a social visit or promenading in the park. But by the turn of the twentieth century, the single-breasted lounge suit was established as the correct outfit for a gentleman to wear during the day.

As we will see in Chapter 3, the Edwardian period was a relatively rich time for menswear, but the First World War marked the end of the old order in many ways, not least in men's styles. After 1918, informality increased. Even in polite society, the frock-coat was rarely seen and the morning coat was usually seen only at weddings, funerals or royal occasions.

Double-breasted suits increased in popularity in the UK at the expense of the waistcoat, but in the late 1920s double-

breasted waistcoats were often worn with single-breasted jackets. Today they are a stylish, if rarely seen, option.

In one of the first examples of a fashion craze, by the mid-1920s 'Oxford bags' appeared among a racy set at the august university. They widened the hems of their trousers to a preposterous twenty-four or twenty-five inches. One theory is that they were modelled on the baggy towelling trousers worn by college rowers over their shorts. Like many crazes, the true 'bags' did not last more than a few years, but men's trousers remained wide until the end of the 1930s.

By the late 1930s, the British look, as dictated by the classic tailoring ideals of Savile Row, continued to set the template for the wardrobe of affluent men worldwide. Not everyone had their suits made by hand – mass manufacturing of ready-made clothes had begun in the late nineteenth century. In the UK a unique phenomenon before 1939 was the rapid growth in the retail empires known as 'multiple tailors', led by Montague Burton, 'The Tailor of Taste'. Born Meshe David Osinsky in 1885, he left what is now Lithuania in 1900 to escape persecution under the Imperial Russian regime. In 1904 he opened a shop as a 'hosier and draper' in Chesterfield, Derbyshire.

Dressing lower-middle-class and working-class men, by 1939 Montague Burton had built up a business that had 595 shops and, in Leeds, the largest men's tailoring factory in the world. Estimates suggested Burton was clothing one-fifth of British men, with ready-made or made-to-measure suits.[6]

After the Second World War, as old social divisions began to break down, some young working-class men wanted to express a new identity. Their costume was to be all-important, as the Teddy Boy craze of the early 1950s showed. The unlikely originators of the look, some people believe, were a group of young Guards officers in the late

1940s, who encouraged their tailors to revive a supposed Edwardian-period look, which comprised a longer jacket with a suppressed or defined waist, flared skirt (the lower part of the jacket) and narrow trousers. Part of their desire was to return to men's dress a correctness that was being eroded by casual clothing imported from America. While this very limited campaign made little impression on the menswear industry, it was given much wider exposure when young working-class Londoners began at first to mimic and then later to exaggerate the style, adding thick crepe-soled shoes and Western-style 'Maverick' ties. In the words of James Laver: 'What was important in this development was not the adoption by the working class of an upper-class style, but the fact that young men from poor backgrounds could now afford relatively expensive clothes and accessories and had the confidence to make them part of their own distinctive style.'[7]

The Teddy Boys were so called because their stylistic inspiration was supposed to be Edward VII. Fashion writer Colin McDowell is not convinced by the myth, arguing:

> ... the Teddy Boy look as a working-class
> restyling of neo-Edwardian dress was largely
> a media invention. In reality, its deeply draped
> jackets, slim-Jim ties and greasily baroque
> hillbilly hairstyles owed more to Hollywood
> than to the West End ... The Teddy Boys, though
> well-publicized, were relatively few in number
> and had no effect at all either on the thousands
> of men in the suburbs who remained content
> with their standardized 'demob' suits or on
> the teenagers and young men happy to dress
> like them.[8]

Yet what the Teddy Boy movement showed was that increasing numbers of young men in Britain were becoming interested in projecting their own identity through their clothes. They wanted their outfits to be noticed; they wanted to dress as a 'tribe' and they were dismissive of, even aggressive towards, other groups that were not part of their tribe. The peacock attitude exemplified by the Teddy Boys' suits and accessories was to be repeated by many youth cults thereafter.

As we will examine in Chapters 7 and 8, the influence of popular music and film has repeatedly redirected the look and language of men's suits. A third element that changed the attitudes to suits – and to all menswear – was the arrival of the youth market as a defined consumer base. In 1957 a twenty-one-year-old Scotsman called John Stephen opened his first shop on Carnaby Street, London, a narrow thoroughfare just two streets away from the home of classic menswear, Savile Row. This enterprise sparked a different attitude towards clothes. They became fashion; they became disposable. They were meant purposely not to last long. In fact, the quality of much that was offered in Carnaby Street was very poor, being produced quickly and inexpensively. But there was so much to choose from – alternatives to plain old grey or dark-blue wool became sought after, worn and accepted. The Peacock Revolution, in which the male of the species ostentatiously showed off his finery after decades of drabness, was starting.

Following quickly after the rise of Carnaby Street – John Stephen alone built up a chain of ten shops, and other businesses such as Lord John followed him – came the importance of Kings Road, Chelsea, as a fashion hot spot. The 1960s fashion queen Mary Quant had opened her first boutique, Bazaar, there in 1955 and the inhabitants of Chelsea offered a well-educated, sociable and affluent consumer base for the new fashion entrepreneurs. The most important pioneer in Chelsea was John Michael Ingram, whose John Michael shops were influential men's boutiques.

Bringing a new blast of creativity close to Savile Row was Rupert Lycett Green, a well-to-do man-about-town who opened a shop called Blades in 1962, which had high tailoring standards but a young man's view of cut and proportion. After five years in Dover Street, Blades relocated to Burlington Gardens, whence its windows commanded a view down Savile Row itself. A tall, elegant, Old Etonian ex-cavalry officer, Lycett Green represented a new sort of entrepreneur that was being attracted to menswear. He told Rodney Bennett England in 1967:

> I had no previous connections with menswear before I opened Blades other than wearing clothes. I was for a while in engineering but was always clothes-conscious. I opened the shop when I was 23 and suppose I was trying to dress people of my own age – certainly under 30 anyway. What I wanted to produce was thin-looking clothes ... The jacket line is high from the chest downwards with long vents. Trousers are flared and have pleatless fronts. I suppose when I started men's fashions were not the big deal they are today. We were perhaps ahead of our time and people thought I was faintly esoteric.[9]

The times were indeed a-changing. Despite the worldwide influence of Swinging London, from the mid-1960s the domination of the London (i.e. Savile Row) look for suits was beginning to be eroded. From the mid-1950s the Italian style – characterised by a tighter, sexier fit for the suit, with narrow trousers and a short 'bum freezer' jacket – had begun to be internationally accepted, notably first in the US. There it was picked up by many showbiz personalities of Italian extraction, such as Rat Pack buddies Frank Sinatra and Dean Martin, who re-exported it to the rest of the world.

> *"My father used to say 'Let them see you and not the suit. That should be secondary'."*
> Cary Grant

Black musicians such as modern jazz trumpeter Miles Davis were fastidious dressers and their adoption of the Italian style was transmuted into the Mod style when it came back to London (named Mod because the look was inspired by Modern Jazz players rather than Trad or Dixieland Jazz players). At the time another influence, now often forgotten, was the trends from Paris, which included a longer, leaner line to the suit, trousers that sat much lower on the hips, and flared trousers, which appeared in the early 1960s although did not gain popular acceptance until the 1970s (see Chapter 6).

The late 1950s and early 1960s were important, too, as the time when designers began to direct the menswear world. No longer were royalty or London's top-class tailors dictating the direction. The pioneers came from the womenswear world – in Paris it was Pierre Cardin and in London Hardy Amies, whose womenswear couture business was based, appropriately, in Savile Row. In 1959 he struck a deal with the British multiple tailor Hepworths to become a style consultant. Amies's far-sighted analysis of the market led to one of the earliest examples of licensing as he put his name on Hepworth's more fashionable suits.

Right: From the late 1960s onwards, there was a wider acceptance of tailoring for women, which inevitably led to his-and-her pairings such as this monochrome duo from 1969.

Not everyone was impressed. At the annual dinner of the Master Tailors Benevolent Association in London, Teddy Watson, tailor to the Duke of Edinburgh, attacked 'the weird and gimmicky garments which have emerged from these people trained and raised in women's dressmaking applying their often absurd ideas to men's tailoring'.[10]

Although many men stuck to the conventional sober suit, the 1960s set the scene for the stylistic variety that we are used to today. Fashion globalisation began as the mass media of movies, music and television were able to bring different looks to the attention of people around the world.

By the late 1960s and early 1970s the suit straddled both convention and fashion. Some men wore suits to work – 'white-collar workers' – because they had to. For manual workers, suits were still the uniform of 'Sunday best' and for smartening themselves up to go out on Friday and Saturday nights. Men wore suits to make an impression on other men and on women; wearing a suit was part of the ritual of dressing up to go out to have fun.

The rise of synthetic fabrics in the 1950s and 1960s brought a new dimension to men's suits. The mixing of polyester and wool, for example, lowered the cost of the fabric and made it more hard-wearing. For the man who *had* to wear a suit for work, rather than *wanted* to wear one, a cheaper, longer-lasting garment was attractive. For the suit purist, however, wool and worsted cloths remained paramount, although adding some mohair was an even more expensive option for those wanting a very sharp image.

Synthetics and synthetic blends were part of the look in the 1970s. Referred to, with some justification, as 'The Decade That Taste Forgot', the 1970s saw men's suits undergoing an extraordinary distortion as shoulders widened, lapels widened, and waists became more pronounced, while trousers were often low-cut, almost skin-tight, with wide flares and deep turn-ups. If these bold shapes were not enough, further attention was drawn to the suit by contrast stitching on a palette of unconventional colours, ranging from the chemically inspired brights to sludgy, earthy tones.

Italian designer Giorgio Armani reinvented the men's suit in the mid-1970s, when he deconstructed the outfit over several seasons (see Chapter 4). Removing much of the unseen inner structure – the interlinings and padding that had traditionally given the jacket form and shape – Armani tapped in to men's contemporary desire for comfort. His approach has probably had the largest single effect on men's suits in the postwar era. Suddenly tailored clothes no longer followed the contours of the body; they were not 'fitted'. While his approach was fashionable, the cachet of his name – and the price of his suits – meant that he quickly became the name of choice for many successful men.

Armani was one of the first after the pioneering Cardin and Amies to be regarded as a menswear 'designer'. By the late 1970s and beyond men who had made their reputation designing women's dresses – such as Yves Saint Laurent, Emanuel Ungaro, Valentino, Louis Féraud – now became directors of style for men. Their names and the licensing deals they made with large suit manufacturers gave a cachet to the sector – suits were definitely a fashion item that could command a premium price. Instead of craftsmen tailors whose styles or 'cut' scarcely changed from one decade to the next, now the market was being driven by international fashion businesses that depended on offering regularly changing ideas.

It was unusual for designers to start their careers in menswear, but a few – such as Nino Cerruti in Italy and France, Ralph Lauren in the US and Paul Smith in the UK –

managed to do so, each having a distinctive 'handwriting' for their suits.

The contrast between suits as a boring uniform for office workers and a discretionary choice for fashion followers was established by the early 1970s and has never disappeared. Whether through unconventional proportions – French designer Jean Paul Gaultier memorably introduced jackets with exaggeratedly wide shoulders and an exaggeratedly tight body in the early 1980s – or through unexpected fabric choices – I recall a fancy suit fabric containing cellophane in the mid-1980s – the demand for novelty in fashion has taken suits a very long way from the correct dimensions of a Savile Row classic.

The 1980s was the decade of the 'power suit', most obviously exemplified by Michael Douglas's character Gordon Gekko in the 1987 movie *Wall Street*. It seemed that you had to be big and brash to carry off a suit with attitude. But simultaneously there was a quickening of the pace of men moving away from suits entirely. The rise of casualwear for leisure time and, more significantly, in the workplace accelerated the decline of the suit.

The 1990s saw the suit come back in fashion, but with a notably minimalist approach, thanks to the stylings of first Austrian designer Helmut Lang and then, soon after, Prada of Italy. Simplicity, functionality and a retreat from any sort of detailing were typical of the uniformly dark suits they produced. There was an almost Beau Brummell-like attention to strict correctness as the silhouette became slim and lean.

The adoption of these suits by the Hollywood elite made them a worldwide phenomenon for the fashion crowd, but many ordinary men still found the entire concept of the suit unappealing. Taking the lead from the laid-back attitude of

Silicon Valley's IT industry, companies began to experiment with 'casual Fridays', when staff could leave their suits at home. Or they embraced the oddly named 'business casual' concept, which meant suits were redundant throughout the entire week. Wearing suits was regarded as something to be avoided. The term 'The Suits' began to be used pejoratively to describe a firm's unpopular senior management team or the boring guys in the accounts department who had no creativity or dress sense.

In the UK, years of adopting casualwear and sportswear for everyday meant that many young men had no suits at all in their wardrobe. In a famously unguarded moment in August 2001, David Shepherd, the man in charge of Topman, the UK's leading chain for young men's fashion, joked to *Menswear* magazine that his customers only bought a suit for their first court appearance before a judge.[11] Yet while many men had no desire for suits, there was a revival on Savile Row, the home of classic tailoring, and in other areas of London, as new names such as Richard James, William Hunt, Timothy Everest, Ozwald Boateng and Nick Hart of Spencer Hart brought a young, fashionable attitude to suits (bespoke or, more commonly, ready-made) – and attracted plenty of celebrity clients.

Pop stars, movie actors, TV celebrities and top sportsmen have replaced royalty as the new arbiters of style, but in a pleasing symmetry of time and style, when they want to announce they have 'arrived' they start wearing suits. The conundrum of the suit remains as potent as ever; ignored by many, revered by many others. There is no sign of the suit disappearing any time soon.

Right: By the mid-1970s, the British multiple tailors were promoting bold fashion looks in suits (not always convincingly, it has to be said). In the mid-1980s Hepworths converted itself into the hugely successful Next chain.

2-piece Crimplene suit, about £26. Credit plan available.

How Hepworths can help relieve those nine-to-five blues.

Above: In the rationed days of post-World War II Britain, likely lads began to express their personality through their clothes. The Teddy Boys, such as this young working-class pair photographed at a fairground in the East End of London in 1955, presented an amalgam of quasi-Edwardian styling and heavy borrowings from American Western looks.

Right: Glaswegian John Stephen came to London in 1957 and opened a shop just two streets from Savile Row in a narrow thoroughfare called Carnaby Street. His approach – to provide affordable, disposable fashion – changed the course of menswear forever. Here he displays the evidence of his success in February 1964.

J. Arthur Rank
Organisation presents

A MICHAEL BALCON PRODUCTION

ALEC GUINNESS
JOAN GREENWOOD
CECIL PARKER in

THE MAN IN THE WHITE SUIT

DIRECTED BY ALEXANDER MACKENDRICK   MADE AT EALING STUDIOS

Above: In this Ealing comedy from 1951, Sidney Stratton (played by Alec Guinness) develops a miracle fabric that will never get dirty or wear out. But it is not produced because of the harm it would do to the clothing industry. Modern technological advances have meant that Stratton's idea is not far from realisation.

Right: For 'If I Can Dream', the final song of his 1968 comeback NBC special, Elvis Presley wore this white suit, designed by Bill Belew, which had distinct echoes of a nineteenth-century outfit for a Southern gentleman. Note the very, very long vents. Belew later designed Elvis' jumpsuit-and-cape stage costumes.

Overleaf: Young Mods Barry Hall, Ken Todd and Brian Hemmings pose with their scooters in 1964. They had clearly absorbed influences from the US and Italy for their stylish look, but obviously had not had time to get their off-the-peg suit sleeves shortened.

The single-breasted suit

Even though it is the most common of suit shapes these days, the single-breasted style offers a huge range of options. The number and the positioning of the buttons is inextricably linked to the length, angle and width of the lapels and so the whole suit 'balances' around the fastening button or buttons.

Far left: TV personality David Frost goes for the one-button style in the early 1960s. The shawl collar is a popular lapel with the single-button fastening.

Centre left: The standard two-button normally fastens only on the top button, as here from the American label Cricketeer in 1970. Two-buttons can be somewhat

dull, but this shows they can also work on a suit with a dash of *élan*. The relatively low fastening permits a long, wide, full lapel.

Centre right: The neat, well-balanced proportions of this Hart Schaffner Marx suit from 1964 show why the three-button style has perennial appeal. The entire outfit is balanced on the centre button, which is the only one that needs fastening.

Far right: Celebrity hairdresser Vidal Sassoon goes his own way in this quintessentially Sixties suit from 1968, designed by Michael St John. He has definitely opted for fashion over convention with this outfit.

chapter TWO
A Question of Balance

The suit is one of the most versatile items in the male wardrobe. Contrary to the criticisms that it is restrictive, boring or anonymous, the suit offers an infinite variety of options in cut, fabric, detail, trimmings and image, as the photographs in this book show. But the devil is indeed in the details.

A good suit is a marvel of geometry, engineering, craft and technical skill, but most of the men who wear it know little of its construction, how or why it fits well, looks good and makes them feel great. For many decades now, most men have known only ready-made suits, bought 'off the peg', to use a quaint old-fashioned phrase. The tradition of the local tailor has died out, particularly in the past forty years. The rarefied bespoke service supplied by Savile Row and a few similar high-class, high-cost tailors in Europe, the US and round the world is available only to a moneyed, powerful elite, led by rich men of commerce, industry and show business, where it once used to be led by royalty and the aristocracy.

It is worth clarifying the difference between the varying types of suit manufacture. At the zenith is the fully bespoke service exemplified by the tailors of Savile Row and the neighbouring streets of Mayfair in London. As menswear commentator James Sherwood has written: 'Bespoke tailoring is a mysterious and secretive art that stands above and beyond all other forms of men's suiting.'[1]

So-called because the customer 'be speaks' what he wants, bespoke tailoring is a totally personal service in which the customer selects his fabric, linings, trimmings, buttons and so on, is personally measured and then the garments are individually cut by hand (by the cutter) and sewn, largely by hand, just for him (by the tailors). Using a complicated system of inner canvases, linings, padding – which are usually sewn by hand – and employing skilful pressing to put shape into the garments, this is five-star service. It is reckoned that at least fifty-two man-hours of work go into the production of a Savile Row bespoke suit. Hand-stitching is reckoned by aficionados to be more precise than machine stitching. More 'give' can be put into the seams and they can, for example, be curved (if required) more accurately than with a machine.

Called 'custom tailoring' in the US, bespoke tailoring has been seen in recent years as the ultimate in luxury purchasing for men; unique clothes made especially and solely for the client – there is little wonder that Savile Row remains an aspirational dream for many suit fans.

Enjoying something of a revival among less well-heeled suit wearers is the service known as 'made-to-measure'. Having been available in some form from the beginning of the 1900s, made-to-measure involves a standard suit pattern or 'block' being amended to fit an individual's measurements before it is made. Again, many fashion companies that sell ready-to-wear suits, even high-level ones, offer this form of personalisation. While it is some way off the unique quality of a full bespoke garment, the customer can choose from a selection of fabrics and the whole process results in a better fit than a simple 'off-the-peg' suit. It offers a degree of exclusivity and in some ways made-to-measure, known as *su misura* in Italian, can be viewed as altering a suit before it is manufactured. Unlike a true bespoke product, however, relatively little handwork goes into a typical made-to-measure suit, but there is a notable improvement in fit.

Among the bespoke fraternity, the omnipresent ready-to-wear suit usually gets a poor rating, but in my view the

Previous page: A 1962 double-breasted suit with peaked lapels is personalised with covered buttons, satin-trimmed turn-back cuffs and, surprisingly, a waistcoat.

sophistication of the modern off-the-peg is a remarkable manifestation of years and years of technical development of fabrics, interlinings, shoulder pads, of assessing the changing dimensions of men's bodies and of producing, consistently, a range of sizes and fits that meet the requirements of many consumers. There is a huge range of differences in the quality of ready-mades. Some use inner canvases to give them shape like bespoke suits; others use heat-sensitive interlinings that are 'fused' to the fabric to give the jacket its inner structure. Even in fused garments, however, there are different qualities and levels of execution. As in most aspects of life, you do tend to get what you pay for. Usually a customer should be prepared to have minor alterations made to an off-the-peg suit; lucky indeed is the man whose ready-to-wear suit fits him perfectly.

The modern manufacturing system that produces consistently high-quality garments at a reasonable price is the result of a more than a hundred years of mass mechanised production. The inch tape measure was not invented until the early 1800s; before that fitting clothes was imprecise by our modern standards. Until the mid-nineteenth century all clothing manufacturing was done by hand, typically in small workshops rather than large factories. Many people who sewed clothing worked at home. By today's standards, the quality of fit, sewing and finish was crude.

In America, the Civil War, which ran from 1861 to 1865, was responsible for speeding up the industrialisation of clothing manufacturing because of the demand for thousands and thousands of uniforms. In the *Esquire Encyclopaedia of 20th-Century Men's Fashion*, the editors highlighted some of the technical developments that contributed to the industrialisation of the clothing sector: the first relatively successful sewing machine (patented 1846 by one Elias Howe); the automatic buttonhole machine

(1862); the button sewer (1875); the bar tack machine (1886); individually powered portable cutting knife to cut multiple layers of fabric (1900); the first pressing machines (1905); a powered vertical knife ten inches long to cut through ever-deeper piles of fabric (1920).[2]

As the *Esquire* writers put it: 'By the end of the nineteenth century was completed the transformation of the (US) industry from the customised concept of apparel manufacturing by hand to the mass production of apparel by machines.' By 1925 the character of apparel manufacturing under industrialised concepts had been definitely formed. In the 1940s practical management – in other words, tailors running the factories – was replaced by professional management. From the 1950s, the changes introduced by the professionals brought a reduction of human labour, a decrease in process time and an improvement of quality.

Europe learned much from the American experience. Huge advances in the techniques of suit production were made after the Second World War. As part of the reconstruction of their shattered infrastructures, both Italy and Germany were able to develop sophisticated modern tailoring systems. From the late 1960s through the 1970s and 1980s, Italy and Germany became major centres for suit production. The menswear industries in Finland, Sweden and Denmark also earned a good reputation for producing modern suits to a high standard. In contrast, the UK and, to a lesser degree, France, suffered from not modernising their infrastructures.

From the 1970s the high labour-cost countries of Western Europe moved their suit production to lower-cost regions, notably Eastern Europe and North Africa; in recent years these areas have lost business to China. The wholesale export of machinery and technical know-how to China has meant that large-scale suit production in Western Europe, apart from at a relatively high-cost level, is rare indeed.

While bespoke tailors make paper patterns and cut each suit by hand using large shears, the most sophisticated factories have for many years used computer-aided design packages and related software that allows them to maximise the use of the fabric. The cutting of up to thirty layers of cloth at a time is achieved through band knives, lasers or even fine jets of highly pressurised water.

Even the tape measure has been superseded by body-scanning techniques. On both sides of the Atlantic, firms are offering a service whereby a man stands in his underwear in a scanning booth. Up to 300,000 data points on the body are logged and used to calculate the circumferences of parts of the body, cross-sectional slice areas, surface areas and volumes. Combined with one-dimensional measurements taken with a trusty tape measure, body scanning is seen as a modern method of addressing the problems of garment fit.

From such measurements, a supposedly better-fitting suit is produced. The German tailoring brand Odermark and the retail chain Brooks Brothers in the US are among the pioneers of the technology. In the 'Digital Tailoring' booths found in selected stores, Brooks Brothers can create in twelve seconds a three-dimensional map of a customer's body through digital scanning. Then a made-to-measure suit that traditionally takes six to eight weeks to make can be completed within fifteen business days for only $100 more than an off-the-peg version.

Whether analysed by the latest white-light digital scanning equipment or the eye of a skilled bespoke cutter, the undeniable fact is that men's bodies vary. Two men with the same chest size or waist size can have significantly different postures, weights, distribution of fat and muscle and, let's face it, personal flair.

The ideal suit is one that will disguise the worst faults and emphasise the best features. Whether going for a classic silhouette or a fashion cut, the key to a suit that will feel comfortable to wear and will win admiration is 'balance'. At its most obvious, this means that the jacket and trousers will be in proportion – a tight-fitting, single-breasted, 1960s-style jacket is complemented best with slim-fitting trousers, of course, while a wide-shouldered, double-breasted, 1930s-style option should be worn with appropriately full-cut trousers.

The nuances of the suit mean that each element is inextricably linked to the next. Each part of the jacket and trousers (and any waistcoat) has to work with the others. The correct 'balance' is achieved when all the elements work in harmony; the angles look correct, the back (with or without vents) complements the front. The geometry of a suit is such that the collar, the lapels and the width of the shoulders define the overall look of the jacket, with the position and size of the armhole finishing the equation.

As the jacket literally hangs from the shoulders, details such as its length, the placement of buttons, the positioning of pockets and the degree of emphasis or 'suppression' on the waist, all fall in place from the shoulder line.

Generally tailor-made suits have much higher and tighter (and therefore smaller) armholes than ready-mades. This means there is less fabric falling from the armholes, which are called scyes in the bespoke trade, so it follows that the jacket literally 'fits' better and does not move as freely as a typical off-the-peg jacket. Ready-made suits have to fit a wide selection of men, so the armholes tend to be larger –

Left: From 1956, a bravura illustration by Luigi Tarquini for Brioni of Rome. The Italian company married superb tailoring excellence with canny marketing skills to achieve a worldwide reputation in the 1950s that lives on today.

a skinny man can get his arms in wide armholes, but a more muscular guy cannot get his arms into narrow armholes.

Many of the key elements of the modern suit are actually redundant. The collar and the lapels or revers serve no practical purpose. Yet to do away with them – as happened for about twenty minutes in the Beatle-suit era of the early 1960s – just does not look right. Similarly, bespoke suits usually have cuff buttons that work, while ready-mades have cuff buttons that are purely decorative.

The height of the collar at the back of a jacket effectively determines the width of the lapels; where these two elements meet on a single-breasted model is at the 'notch'. The only single-breasted lapel not to have a notch is the shawl collar, which runs unbroken from the collar to the buttons – it is rarely seen outside of evening wear.

Along with the collar and the lapels, the pockets of a jacket influence the overall impression. Patch pockets, formed when a rectangle of fabric is sewn on the outside of the jacket, are the most casual of all. Flapped pockets are surprisingly versatile; they can be rather dull when, as is normal, they sit horizontally, but they offer a rakish appeal when they are set at an angle. Most suit wearers are happy with two hip pockets, but traditionalists and fashion followers alike prefer a third 'ticket' pocket on the right.

For a clean line on body-skimming or minimalist jackets, jetted or besom pockets are preferred. These are simply a neatly finished slit in the fabric; they are very slick when executed correctly.

Trousers are perhaps even more remarkable than jackets in their ability to cover such a bizarre set of contours as the lower part of a man's body. A defining measurement for determining the look of a trouser is the 'rise' – that is, the distance from the crotch to the waistband. Traditional bespoke trousers have a rise of ten or twelve inches; some extreme, modern, low-rise trousers may cover only five or six inches. Classic trousers were held up with braces; belts or nothing are the widely preferred option today. Pleats are used to gather the excess fabric on wider-cut trousers; they can number one or two, and can face inwards or outwards. They help when a man's body is not as slim as it used to be, but for a clean line you cannot beat a plain-fronted trouser, that is, one without pleats.

The width of the trouser is largely determined by the fullness of the cut around the backside and hips. Over the years men have tried everything from the skin-tight 'drainpipe' to the eccentric ultra-wide 'Oxford bags'. Again the desire for 'balance' in the suit should guide the wearer, along with his body shape and height. A curse of the ready-to-wear suit is overlong trousers. Some people favour trousers to 'break' or reach just to the shoe, or even slightly above it, but surely no one wants a concertina-type effect of fabric crumpled up at the bottom of the trouser. Yet this is too often the effect with off-the-peg trousers being made long so they can be taken up to the correct length – too many men cannot be bothered to attend to this minor chore.

Out of favour on fashion suits for quite some time now are turn-ups (or 'cuffs' if you are American). Called PTUs in the business (for Permanent Turn-Ups), they can add a neat line of definition at the hem of the legs, while also usefully adding a touch of weight to hold down a wider trouser.

One important consideration with trousers, whether off-the-peg or bespoke: always buy a second pair when you acquire your suit, as trousers wear out a lot faster than jackets and a second pair is a very sensible investment if you want to prolong the active life of your ensemble.

Above: In the late 1970s and early 1980s Hugo Boss combined German technical efficiency with Italian styling and American marketing techniques to become the best-known of the many excellent German suit producers. American model Michael Flynn (centre) became the face of the company for several years.

Pockets, too, offer a surprising number of options – the familiar slanting side pockets are the most common entry to relatively deep pouches. I like the vertical entry of a 'frogmouth' pocket, which runs horizontally, parallel to the waistband. For a really tight-fitting pair of trousers you can do away with pockets entirely, although this is an option taken up only by the like of tango dancers ...

Back pockets come in three options: two, one or none. Flapped, jetted or buttoned closures are the usual options – and they can be mixed on a pair of trousers.

Along with the 'rise', another useful measurement in men's suits is the 'drop', which is the term given to the difference between a man's chest measurement and his waist measurement. In most cases this is rarely more than six inches, so off-the-peg suits are manufactured accordingly. To get round the problem of men who are exceptionally

well muscled – and so have a very full chest and a tight waist – and those who are anything but – and so have a chest and waist measurement that is almost the same, many ready-to-wear companies offer 'mix-and-match' suits. Here a jacket and a trouser in the same fabric can be bought separately to produce a better overall impression for the man who does not meet the average requirements.

Sir Hardy Amies, always a champion of traditional English tailoring, made a provocative point in his book *The Englishman's Suit*, when he challenged the idea that a suit could be redesigned:

> *I feel there ought to be a word other than 'designer' for a 'designer' of men's suits. You cannot truly design or redesign a garment, the basic shape of which is already determined by history. If you don't follow tradition in design of a suit inherited from the past, you have no suit. A 'designer' can alter proportions: of length of coat, of width of shoulder, of placing of buttons. He can propose a double-breasted instead of a single-breasted fastening. But he is not 'designing' a suit; he is very often only proposing to alter details of a suit which already exists.*[3]

Leaving aside personal requirements, there are some general rules of wearing suits that apply no matter what the provenance of the garments. For smaller than average men, the received wisdom is to stay away from patterns and wear smooth worsted cloths. More 'meaty' fabrics such as flannels or tweeds are relatively thick and so make the wearer look thick-set. Stripes, especially narrowly placed stripes, help to give the impression of height as the observer's eyes move up and down. Checks, conversely, encourage the eyes to move horizontally, giving the impression of width, not height. For the small man, a solid, smooth fabric is often the best option.

A tighter fit is recommended too. Small actors such as Edward G Robinson, James Cagney and Alan Ladd always wore suits with as little superfluous cloth as they could bear, because bagginess adds width, which undermines height. Jackets need to be no longer than sufficient to cover the backside as too-long jackets cover the legs and reduce the impression of height. A hint of a waist, provided by some 'suppression', to use the jargon, is preferable to a jacket hanging straight, and the waist and fastening button ought to be relatively high, something near halfway up from the hem of the jacket.

To add to the impression of lengthening the body, the waist of the trousers needs to be at the natural waist, which means at the belly button or above. Ventless jackets, which are regarded as the most slimming option, are also recommended for the small guy.

The choice of the number of buttons makes for a fascinating discussion. Very elegant, but suited best to tall, slim men with excellent posture, is the single-button option. The uncluttered front of the jacket is elongating in itself. The single button is being seen on more high-class fashionable suits these days, but most men only risk it on evening wear, as it has a dressy look.

Two-buttoned jackets are a very popular choice; without a top third button, the lapel can be longer, elongating the silhouette. Normally only the upper of the two buttons is closed. Some men dislike the two-button option, as it can be lacking in flair; it's a bit ordinary.

Left: *The Avengers* was recorded from 1961 to 1969. John Steed (played by Patrick MacNee) was the only ever-present character in the series and played the well-tailored Englishman gentleman to an audience around the world. Reportedly, he designed his outfits himself. Here, note the lack of a breast pocket.

Three-buttoned jackets offer more ways to get it right – and an equal number to get it wrong. If the top button is meant to be fastened, then the lapels have to be shorter. But a more elegant option is the three-button in which only the middle button is used. Often the length and roll of the lapel means that the top button cannot be used – like many other features on the suit, it is redundant and purely decorative.

In recent years there has been a trend in off-the-peg suits to have suits in which all three buttons should be closed. On many men this gives the impression that the suit jacket is a tube – it is, to my eyes, a displeasing look, especially when a fourth or even a fifth button is added. The high-fastening front means that only a small area of shirt and tie is left to relieve the expanse of jacket.

The general advice is that smaller men should not wear a double-breasted (or DB) suit, as the extra cloth across the stomach – known as the 'wrap' or the 'crossover' – increases the appearance of girth, as do the two lines of buttons. But I think it depends on the man and how he carries himself. That applies to many so-called 'rules' for good dressing.

Between the single-breasted (SB) and DB styles there are some opportunities to exchange characteristics. Much in vogue recently have been DB lapels on an SB jacket. This gives a stylish look of flair, providing the impression of wide shoulders above a trim torso, so it works well on younger men.

Just as the number of buttons on an SB suit can define its overall look, so the number and positioning of the two rows of buttons on a DB are crucial to its overall effect. The classic arrangement is for three buttons on each side, in which the lower and middle left-hand buttons fasten, while the upper button does not. The middle button should be set just above the waistline. The two upper buttons are traditionally set wider than the lower pairs to suggest a V-shape moving towards the shoulders, an impression that is encouraged by the peaked lapel of a DB jacket. Over the years there have been attempts to distort this classic shape, but with little success. A narrow six-button arrangement in which all three buttons fasten can look good, although it does have a retro air.

A DB with only four or, even worse, only two buttons rarely looks attractive. In the early 1980s, a fashion trend from Italy had the fastening buttons very low-set, in some cases notably below the waistline. I'm with Sir Hardy Amies on this one: '[The Italians'] boldest move was to bypass the waist altogether and place a button several inches below it. It certainly emphasised a lower waistline and immediately made the double-breasted coat (jacket) look less stuffy, but – and it's a big but – it does shout "off the peg". I do not think a truly stylish Italian gentleman would wear the button placed so near his genitalia.'[4]

DB suits almost always carry peaked lapels – the notched lapel more commonly seen on an SB looks totally wrong in the DB format – but within that limitation, there are a variety of widths and angles. The super-wide lapels of the 1930s 'gangster' suit are sported only rarely today, usually by extrovert vintage-fashion fans. Once again, the width and angle of the DB lapels contribute to the 'balance' of the suit.

Handbooks on dressing are, appropriately, full of advice on what different men should wear. Nicholas Antongiavanni in *The Suit* advises the taller person thus:

> *The tall man should never wear skimpy or tight-fitting clothes, for they only make him look leaner and thus taller, as do jackets with square, built-up shoulders or narrow lapels, or that have no vents, or that do not cover his seat; and nothing contributes more to a tall man's ruin than a short jacket.*[5]

I'm not sure I agree with the apparent premise that the tall man does not wish to emphasise his height; the recommendations seem more appropriate for the more-than-averagely skinny man. Being a traditionalist, Antongiavanni recommends DBs for the tall gent, but suggests that only the waist button be fastened, not the bottom one. Again, to add fullness and width, he recommends that the two hip pockets and the ticket pocket are flapped and – the mark of a classicist – that the trousers have turn-ups or 'cuffs'. He also recommends pleats on the trousers to add to the appearance of fullness across the horizontal axis. He encourages tall men to wear checks and windowpanes, rather than dark plains, to give the optical illusion of a wider dimension. American designer and menswear expert Alan Flusser's books are also exhaustive in their advice on selecting a suit to best enhance body shape, complexion, hair colour and so on.

A real fan of the suit will be the man most likely these days to still champion the waistcoat – known as the 'vest' by bespoke tailors and Americans. Once worn for extra warmth and for decency (so the body was still covered when the jacket was open), the waistcoat fell out of favour after the Second World War. The popularity of DB jackets in the 1930s heralded the waistcoat's decline, but improvements in heating in buildings and the rise of car ownership contributed to its demise. It's a shame, because a waistcoat can lift a suit to a higher level of elegance. It looks particularly striking when it carries its own neat revers. A very confident man will go for the DB waistcoat – Steve McQueen memorably wore more than one in *The Thomas Crown Affair* in 1968. You'll be lucky to find many ready-to-

Right: By 1964, the lines of a man's suit had been slimmed down to the elegant proportions of this three-button SB from Aquascutum. Marketing to men was also increasingly important, hence the growth of striking images such as this one.

Above: London showbiz tailor Dougie Millings adapted the Pierre Cardin look to dress the Fab Four in their iconic Beatle suits. In fact, they wore this look for a relatively short time from 1962, before moving onto more conventional suits.

Left: Pop and rock stars formed the high-profile backbone of the clientele for Tommy Nutter, seen here in November 1969. He brought a blast of fashion to the hallowed pavements of Savile Row, while maintaining the highest tailoring standards.

wear brands offering a waistcoat today, so to acquire one you will have to go made-to-measure or bespoke. Convention decrees that the bottom button of the waistcoat is left unfastened. It's all part of the suit tradition.

Remember, also, that the suit you choose should also determine the size and shape of your shirt collar and, by extension, the size of your tie knot. It's all about that question of 'balance' again. It's very acceptable to dress down your suit with a polo-neck sweater or a fine polo shirt and these days a suit worn without a tie is seen every day. Not for the first time, this is a development that would not have won the approval of the late Sir Hardy Amies. Ever the traditionalist, he wrote: 'A suit without a tie looks awful.'[6]

Opposite: British tailoring absorbed a significant influx of craftsmen when immigration from the Caribbean began in the 1940s. West Indians also brought a swaggering sense of style that has enriched British menswear ever since. For these three Jamaican immigrants, John Hazel, Harold Wilmot and John Richards, pictured on the first immigration ship, the *Empire Windrush*, in June 1948, the US zoot-suit influence on their outfits is obvious (see p. 100).

Left: Formerly Terry Nelhams from Acton, West London, British pop star Adam Faith was a pin-up both for girls and for Mod boys. This Italian-influenced mohair or silk SB was the height of 1963 pop style.

"*In fashion today
there are no old men;
only the young and the dead.*"

Hardy Amies,

An ABC of Men's Fashion (1964)

Right: The Men from U.N.C.L.E., Napoleon Solo (Robert Vaughan) and Illya Kuryakin (David McCullum) were among the best-dressed heroes of the small screen from 1964 to 1968. Appropriately, they usually entered their HQ in New York by a secret door in Del Floria's Tailor Shop. And, no, we have no idea why Napoleon Solo is wearing clogs here!

Overleaf: A splendid line-up of men's tailoring styles from the City of London in 1931 – note the subtle variations in the apparently similar styles. The fabric mills must have loved those wide trousers, wide lapels and waistcoats.

The double-breasted suit

The 'wrap' of a DB suit, covering from one side of the body to the other, harks back to the ancestor of the suit, the frock coat. More difficult to tailor and often more difficult to wear, the DB suit represents for many the epitome of masculine style.

Far left: The high crossover on Humphrey Bogart's suit, from the 1937 film *Kid Galahad*, leaves little room for a display of shirt and tie. The glen check is a brave choice; note the difficulty in making the checks match from sleeve to chest.

Centre left: Many buttons on a DB can often be largely decorative, as here on a Jean Paul Gaultier suit from Spring/Summer 1998.

Centre right: On this fanciful creation from Pierre Cardin in 1968, note the angles of the relatively short but wide lapels and the large collar, and the narrowing effect of the four buttons being close together. The striped fabric only adds to the optical effect.

Far right: Simple and sleek, Clint Eastwood's six-button suit seems to have won the approval of French actress Jean Seberg at a cast party for *Paint Your Wagon* (1969), in which they starred together.

chapter THREE
Princes Among Men

Until the middle of the twentieth century, English royalty set the standards of dress for gentlemen the world over. The most influential royals of the past hundred years were both known as Edward, Prince of Wales, and both had something bordering on an obsession for clothes.

The man who became King Edward VII was the first menswear icon to be seen regularly by the general public. The second child and eldest son of Queen Victoria and Prince Albert was born on 9 November 1841, just two years after the first daguerreotype had been made public. His parents became avid devotees of the new photographic technology and their already lofty standing in the world was further elevated by the fact that now their millions of subjects could see what they looked like.

Albert Edward – always known as Bertie to his family – was born to a mother who was only twenty-two, but who had already been queen for four years. His sister Vicky had been born the previous November. By December 1841 the infant boy had been created Prince of Wales, the title that would be associated with him for nearly sixty years until his mother's death in 1901. Edward straddled two centuries, as the bridge between the Victorian Age and the modern day. He was still in his teens when he began to make the foreign trips that were to give him an international profile. Italy was on the schedule in 1859 and North America in 1860. He was an internationally recognised playboy prince and, in contrast to his severe father and his long-grieving mother, Edward enjoyed his clothes. He had a huge influence on what men wore; he was an unrivalled ambassador for the English tailoring elite, and, given his enthusiastic womanising, he enabled men to like clothes without worrying about accusations of effeminacy.

In 1858, aged seventeen, he was given an allowance of £500 (which equates to about £40,000 in today's money), mainly to buy his own clothes, but his parents were anxious he understood his station in life. His father was already worried about him and wrote to a family member: 'Unfortunately he takes no interest in anything but clothes, and again clothes. Even when out shooting, he is more occupied with his trousers than with the game!'[1]

His mother was concerned that the prince presented himself correctly and wrote to him (in words that may have been her husband's):

> I must say now that we do not wish to control
> your own tastes and fancies which, on the
> contrary, we wish you to indulge and develop,
> but we do expect that you will never wear
> anything extravagant or slang, not because we
> don't like it, but because it would prove a want
> of self-respect and be an offence against decency,
> leading as it has often done before in others,
> to an indifference to what is morally wrong.[2]

Prince Albert, ever anxious that things should be correct, laid down the law on his son's dress for the benefit of the men appointed to attend on the young prince:

> The appearance, deportment and dress of a
> gentleman consist perhaps more in the absence of
> certain offences against good taste, and in careful
> avoidance of vulgarities and exaggerations of any
> kind, however generally they may be the fashion
> of the day, than in the adherence to any rules
> which can be exactly laid down ... In dress, with
> scrupulous attention to neatness and good taste,
> he will never give in to the unfortunately loose
> and slang style which predominates at the
> present day. He will borrow nothing from the
> fashion of the groom or the gamekeeper, and

*whilst avoiding the frivolity and foolish vanity
of dandyism, will take care that his clothes are
of the best quality, well-made, and suitable to
his rank and position ... To all these particulars
the Prince of Wales must necessarily pay more
attention than anyone else. His deportment
will be more watched, his dress more criticised.*[3]

These comments summed up how virtually all Englishmen of
breeding viewed matters of dress. As he entered adulthood,
however, Edward reacted against his strict upbringing and
began enjoying the finer things of life, such as cigars,
hunting, women and the company of a racy set – his days of
fast living had begun. A liaison with an Irish actress called
Nellie Clifden caused a scandal and the family believed the
stress contributed to Prince Albert's early death in 1861.

It was Albert's wish that his son should wed young and so it
was that Edward was married to Alexandra, a Danish
princess, on 10 March 1863. He was awarded an income of
around £100,000 (more than £7 million at today's values)
and began to live the life of an aristocrat to the full. His
mother had a low opinion of his abilities for royal duties and
was nervous about some of his associates, so Edward had
few formal responsibilities to distract him from the life of a
privileged playboy.

He was bored and his gambling and attendance at race
meetings amused him. 'He preferred men to books and
women to either,' was one summation of the Prince.

Previous page: Edward, Prince of Wales, in the early 1920s, championing the
'dress soft' approach that was one of his lasting legacies.

Right: Photographed in about 1890, the best international advertisement for English
tailoring, the future Edward VII always looked smart, despite his ample frame.

Even while in his late teens, Edward adopted Henry Poole at 36 Savile Row as his tailor after admiring the cut of an outfit worn by an actor when he attended the theatre. In 1860 the initial order from the young prince was for a short smoking jacket – it was, in fact, the first modern dinner jacket. Later, so one story goes, one of his American guests took back a similarly styled jacket to the Tuxedo Park club in New York, where it was immediately adopted as fashionable evening wear by club members, becoming known in the US as a tuxedo.

The links between Henry Poole and Edward gave the tailor unrivalled access to the world's ruling elite. Poole made a suit for the Japanese ambassador to Queen Victoria's court – ever since, the Japanese word for a suit has been *sebiro* (or *sabiro*), the nearest pronunciation they can get to 'Savile Row'.

As the nineteenth century wore on and Queen Victoria rarely moved from her widow's home on the Isle of Wight, Edward made official visits to places as far away as Egypt in 1869 and India in 1875. He made frequent visits to France – to Paris, Cannes, the Riviera and Biarritz, and high society in France readily adopted fashion from *le Prince de Galles*. He was a highly effective ambassador for *le style Anglais*. In the words of his stylish successor, the Duke of Windsor: 'He was a good friend to Savile Row, consolidating the position of London as the international sartorial shrine for men.'[4] As Colin McDowell has observed: 'Edward stimulated the belief that Savile Row alone knew how to tailor with the degree of perfection required by a gentleman.'[5]

When he travelled abroad, Edward was accompanied by trunks carrying more than forty suits and twenty pairs of shoes.[6] At resorts and spas such as Homburg and Marienbad in Germany, tailors from across Europe followed him, photographing his latest outfits and making notes. Despite being short in stature and increasingly fat, he rarely looked anything but impeccably dressed. When he got so fat that

a DB frock-coat was unsuitable, he wore a frock-coat with an SB fastening but DB peaked lapels.

By the 1890s Edward's habits of dress – he could change up to six times a day – set the trends for the smart set. Among his innovations were the black Homburg hat (brought back from a trip from the German spa), the dinner jacket, shorter tails on evening wear, creases at the side of trousers not the front, the adoption of turn-ups on trousers (to protect the bottoms from muddy ground), the wearing of tweeds at race meetings and, some suggest, leaving open the button on a waistcoat. According to the Duke of Windsor, for a while Edward wore velvet suits for tea, favouring colours as bright as turquoise blue, emerald green and crimson. But when the homosexual Oscar Wilde gave lectures while wearing a velvet suit, the prince desisted rapidly.[7] Even a man whose name had been linked with a list of beauties such as Sarah Bernhardt, Lillie Langtry, the Hon. Mrs George Keppel, Frances, Countess of Warwick and a dancer at the Moulin Rouge did not want to be associated with homosexuality.

Edward VII's greatest legacy to menswear was to promote the idea of practical elegance. This was seen most pertinently in his sporting clothes. Game shooting was one of the Prince's greatest passions. At the royal estate in Sandringham in Norfolk there were regular pheasant and partridge shoots, while at Abergeldie Castle near Balmoral in Scotland deer stalking was enjoyed. In a desire to have a practical jacket that allowed him to be comfortable while shooting, he endorsed the Norfolk jacket. Its belt and vertical pleats soon became familiar across the world.

Edward was also a keen yachtsman and golfer, but his favourite sport was horse racing, literally 'the sport of kings'. One critic noted that he attended twenty-eight race meetings in 1890, nearly three times as many days as he attended the House of Lords. He was a successful racehorse

Above: The 1981 TV adaptation of *Brideshead Revisited* re-introduced the British aristocratic look to a new audience. A huge hit in the US, Bloomingdale's built a successful promotion around the series, which starred Anthony Andrews.

owner (in 1896 his horse Persimmon won the Derby) and the crowds that mobbed him at the racecourses shouted 'good old Teddy'; fifty years later, in memory of his image, his nickname was adopted by the Teddy Boys.

Despite his attention to detail in dress, Edward was eager to simplify the prevailing dress codes. At Sandringham, for example, he decreed that it was not necessary for his guests to change the usual four times a day – the rota had been first morning suit, then hunting clothes for the chase, followed by morning suit during the afternoon, and finally evening dress for dinner. The Prince let it be known that in Norfolk he was happy with only two outfits – shooting tweeds for day and evening dress for dinner.

When Queen Victoria died on 22 January 1901, her son and heir was a little over fifty-nine years old. Once king, he

quickly established Buckingham Palace as the main royal residence and ruled at the apex of the London social pyramid. Accounts of the sovereign's activities became regular features of popular newspapers. He was an unlikely style icon; shortly before his coronation, the royal waist was forty-eight inches, about the same as his chest. He had a huge appetite. One memorable dinner ran to twenty courses; his ordinary meals often involved twelve dishes.

Due to his vast network of relatives, Edward became known as 'the uncle of Europe'. A stickler for correctness in dress, he could also be a snob; he disliked the American sense of dress, bright ties and extravagant waistcoats and dismissed the Portuguese nobility as resembling 'waiters in a second-class restaurant'.

To today's eyes, Edward VII makes an unlikely pin-up. As Colin McDowell has observed: 'Today it is inconceivable that a portly man, well into middle age, could generate such a fuss, but in the early years of the century, kings were considered glamorous because, in a male-dominated society, they were still viewed as fathers of nations, leaders of empires and rulers of men. Their dress was automatically seen as the garb of power and therefore of interest to all men.'

The king died on 6 May 1910 and *Men's Wear* magazine recalled that 'his gaiety and readiness for colour and change had done much for the men's wear trade'.[8] Prince von Bulow, the German Chancellor, summed up his reputation succinctly: 'In the country in which unquestionably the gentlemen dressed best, he was the best-dressed gentleman.'[9]

Even more influential than Edward VII was his grandson, the man who was, albeit briefly, Edward VIII. Edward Albert Christian George Andrew Patrick David was born on 23 June 1894. Known to the family as David, he was nearly sixteen when his grandfather Edward VII died and his father came to the throne as George V. In a strange contradiction of the maxim 'like father, like son', George had little interest in clothes or fashion. His son, the young Prince of Wales, more than compensated.

Thanks to the increased use of photography, he became an even bigger celebrity than Edward VII. 'Photography, killing the private life of princes ... made me familiar to all,' he wrote in a 1960 memoir, *A Family Album*:

> After World War I the privacy which had traditionally enshrouded royalty was considerably diminished. Before the turn of the century royalty was not portrayed off guard. By 1918 the development of the high-speed shutter, improved techniques of artificial lighting and highly sensitive films made it possible to invade the privacy of all public figures. Radio, newsreels and later television brought the voices and images of royalty into every home.[10]

Echoing the position of his grandfather towards Prince Albert and Queen Victoria, the Prince of Wales was in almost constant conflict with his old-fashioned, duty-bound parents, especially the king. It has been suggested that many of his stylistic innovations were introduced just to annoy his father. He claimed not to be clothes-obsessed: 'Let it not be assumed that clothes have ever been a fetish of mine. Rather, I have become, by force of circumstances and upbringing, clothes-conscious. My position as Prince of Wales dictated that I should always be well and suitably dressed for every conceivable occasion,' he wrote in 1960.

Edward was the most widely travelled, most photographed and most admired member of the royal family between the end of the First World War and the beginning of 1936 when George V died. He seemed typical of the young men who had survived the horrors of the war and were determined to disregard the strictures and formality of the older generation.

'It was not of course until after the First World War that it became possible for a man to display anything like an individual taste in dress,' he said.

> All my life I had been fretting against those constrictions of dress which reflected my family's world of rigid social convention ... Comfort and freedom were the two principles that underlay the change in male fashions throughout the freer and easier democratic age between the First World War and the Second. It was a change, however, which after the manner of the conservative male, happened gradually ... in a sense, imperceptibly.[11]

Like his grandfather, Edward's role was to act as an ambassador for Britain around the world: he became known as 'the hardest-working commercial traveller in the service of the Empire'. As he observed:

> All the smart young men of the period were used by the clothing industry as unconscious models for the propagation of British fashions and the sale of British products all over the world, and especially in America. I myself played a fairly prominent and for the most part unconscious role in this process. After all it was part of my job as Prince of Wales to support and to stimulate British trade in general, and this inevitably includes men's clothes.

Right: The Prince of Wales' love of the sporting life determined that his clothing was made more comfortable and easy to move in. This photo dates from 1893.

Above: The future Emperor Hirohito (right) displayed the global appeal of the British look during the Prince of Wales' tour of Japan in 1926.

I am credited with having influenced styles in my time. It was quite unconscious; I have always tried to dress to my own individual taste ... I was in fact produced as a leader of fashion, with my clothiers as my showmen and the world as my audience. The middle man in this process was the photographer, employed not only by the Press but by the trade, whose task it was to photograph me on every possible occasion, public or private, with an especial eye for what I happened to be wearing. A selection of these photographs, together with patterns and materials and samples of collars, ties, socks, waistcoats, and so forth, was immediately rushed to America, where overnight a new fashion might well be born – to the considerable advantage of the British export trade.[12]

While Edward wondered 'whether in the eyes of certain sections of the Press I was not more of a glorified clothes-peg than the heir-apparent', it became clear that what he wore often, though not always, became fashionable.

Sometimes his penchant for bold colours and clashing patterns – such as checked suit, checked shirt, striped tie, patterned pocket handkerchief and two-tone shoes – were too dissonant to be truly tasteful.

Yet, in the 1920s and 1930s, he was the brightest and best-looking royal star – blond, blue-eyed, at five-foot-five a little too short to be an imposing figure, but lively, amusing, articulate and very keen on the close company of women. His vast travelling wardrobe was transported in no fewer than forty tin trunks, supervised by his valet Jack Crisp.

Among his credits are making the double-breasted suit acceptable daytime wear for gentlemen. In his desire for comfort, or, as he put it, to 'dress soft', he liked unlined suit jackets and sports jackets. He wore co-respondent shoes (which George V deplored as the mark of a bounder or cad) and suede shoes, which, before Edward's patronage, were usually regarded as footwear worn only by homosexuals. He wore his brown suede shoes with a navy-blue suit, which was virtually unheard of. Following the American example, he preferred belts to braces on his trousers. In September 1935 the British trade magazine *Men's Wear* felt its readers ought to know that the Prince had been seen in Cannes wearing both trousers and shorts with a zipper rather than a button fly. George V deplored this uncouth innovation.

On the golf course, Edward continued the revival of plus-fours, a style of knickerbockers that allowed fabric to hang four inches below the knee. He introduced midnight blue as a colour for evening suits, mainly because subtle details such as lapels, buttons and pockets showed up better in photographs than they did on a black suit.

Not everything given Edward's name was strictly his creation. The large 'Windsor' knot for a tie was, in fact, never worn by him; his large tie knots were formed because he had especially thick ties made for him by Hawes and Curtis in London. Similarly, the 'Prince of Wales' check was not made for him; it is more properly a variant of a Glenurquhart district check from Scotland that had been around since the 1840s. Indeed, Edward VII had often worn it in his day.

For forty years, from 1919 to 1959, the prince patronised the firm of the Dutchman Frederick Scholte, just off Savile Row, almost always visiting the tailor at his shop. ('I cannot imagine King George V in a London shop,' he mused.) Basing his suit-jacket shape on the tunic of Guards officers, Scholte had developed 'The London Cut' or 'The Drape', which had broad shoulders narrowing from the arms to the waist. The prince had his jacket waists set high to elongate his silhouette. Scholte's cut was very influential in Europe and especially in America, where it developed into the 1930s' four-button DB longer jackets with less waist emphasis.

Showing a typical contrariness, the prince never had trousers made by Scholte, preferring instead to have them supplied by Forster & Son in London or H Harris, a New York tailor who had served an apprenticeship in London. Both cut trousers to be worn with a belt, not braces. Edward's pockets were cut wider on the left side of the trousers to accommodate his ever-present cigarette case. Having been obsessed with his weight when a young man, he had elasticised girdles inset beneath his waistband to preserve the flat appearance of his stomach.

After his abdication in 1936, the British menswear industry lost its most dominating personality. With his wife Wallis Simpson, the Duke of Windsor, as he became, remained a favourite of the popular press until his death on 28 May 1972.

A 1960 inventory of the Duke of Windsor's wardrobe listed fifteen evening suits, fifty-five lounge suits and three formal suits (all with two pairs of trousers), along with more than a hundred pairs of shoes. Many of the suits were auctioned by Sotheby's in New York in 1998; most of the interest came from outside the UK, with the upmarket Italian firm Kiton paying $110,000 for eleven items. The Roman firm Brioni also bought several items.

Since Edward was shipped into exile no man in the British royal family has either wanted or dared to show the same interest in clothes. Edward's brother King George VI appeared to wear clothes to suit the role that was thrust upon him, rather than enjoying them for his own sake. His grandson, Charles, the current Prince of Wales, who was born on 14 November 1948, often looked uncomfortable in formal clothes until 1981, when his new wife Princess Diana encouraged him to acquire his suits from Anderson & Sheppard of Savile Row. Previously, Charles, in the best tradition of the aristocracy, had gone to Hawes and Curtis, the tailor of his father, the Duke of Edinburgh, and had been guided in matters sartorial by his valet Stephen Barry. From Anderson & Sheppard, the heir apparent acquires his seemingly ubiquitous DB 'drape' suits that echo Scholte's cut of almost a hundred years ago.

Today the members of the British royal family dress conservatively, safely and often in an unashamedly old-fashioned way, but at least the Prince of Wales, with his long torso and slightly short legs, looks comfortable in his suits. American menswear writer Nicholas Antongiavanni approves: 'In our time Charles is the most visible representative of the Drape ... When you see him, notice above all other factors that subtle amount of superfluous cloth in the chest and blades: that is the drape. And notice how his suit does not look stiff and starchy but always softy and supple.'[13]

His two famous predecessors as Prince of Wales probably approve of this modern royal style.

Above: Prince Charles can never be faulted in his formal clothes and this is a particularly fine example of a three-piece morning suit. He wore it to the wedding of Princess Alexia of Greece to Carlos Morales Quintana in July 1999, but it would have been perfectly acceptable a hundred years earlier.

Right: Anderson & Sheppard tailors the Prince of Wales' ubiquitous double-breasted drape suits. He has found a style he likes and wears it everywhere – even for a stroll through a vegetable patch.

Above: Paul Smith takes the applause for his Autumn/Winter 1988 catwalk show in a modern interpretation of the three-piece country suit.

Left: An impeccable Edward VII (far left) takes a purposeful stroll in Marienbad, Germany, in 1906, with his courtiers Sir Stanley Clarke and Major Frederick Ponsonby.

Above: Modern designers cannot resist re-interpreting the royal checked look. Here's a bright idea from Vivienne Westwood's collection for Autumn/Winter 2001.

Right: The seventy-year-old Duke of Windsor photographed at his home in Paris in 1964 in a typically bold suit that might have been forty years old.

The striped suit

Only the wildest eccentric would ever wear a suit of horizontal stripes. Vertical stripes, however, are popular mainly because they give the effect of lengthening the wearer's body. They also allow a touch of personality or colour in what is essentially a conventional outfit.

Far left: In *Marriage Italian-Style* (1964), Marcello Mastroianni showed the stylish possibilities of a three-piece with narrowly set chalk stripes. These popular stripes are so named because they represent the marks made on cloth by tailor's chalk.

Centre left: Proving that a striped suit can be subversive, Brian Jones of The Rolling Stones wore this striking number for a court appearance in June 1967.

Centre right: Always the best-dressed Stone, drummer Charlie Watts, on a US tour in 1975, wears a summery DB that reverses Brian Jones' stripes.

Far right: From the Swedish manufacturer Widengrens in 1976, this is a fine example of a bold fancy stripe, for the man who really wants to be noticed.

chapter FOUR

The Italian Job

Italy's influence on menswear, which has been so significant during the past fifty years, has a lengthy history. It had certainly been noticed by the late 1600s when William Shakespeare alluded to it in *Richard II,* which itself was set in the late 1300s. The Duke of York's criticism of Richard's courtiers copying the styles from Italy was echoed from the 1950s onwards by foreign menswear traditionalists when Italy's suit manufacturers began to export beyond the Alps.

Appropriately for a nation that became more or less unified only in the 1860s and 1870s, Italy has always had regional differences in its approach to tailoring. Milan, now the centre of international menswear, had the reputation for discreet, even serious tailoring along the lines of the British. At the other extreme, Naples was famous for its *guapa* or showy southern style and its tailors' ability to make lightweight suits. Rome was less flashy than Naples and more inventive than Milan. Reportedly, there were 100,000 tailors working in post-war Italy, who at that time dressed an estimated 85 per cent of the adult male population. It was all the more remarkable, then, that the Italians became the leading manufacturers of high-quality ready-made suits in the modern era, as well as among the most effective modern marketers.

Sometimes it takes a geo-political conflict to change the face of fashion. In the mid-1970s the fallout from the Arab-Israeli struggle left the developed world feeling scared, flat and disinclined to buy suits as the price of oil soared. In 1975 the huge Italian tailoring manufacturer Gruppo Finanzario Tessile, known as GFT, found that its business had stalled. 'In the first ten days of our seasonal selling campaign to the menswear business, we had sold nothing,'

Carlo Rivetti, whose family had built up the Turin-based GFT, told me in 2008. 'We had a good reputation and good products but it wasn't enough and we knew we had to add something to our offer to rejuvenate our business. My cousin Marco Rivetti had an idea of doing a new line with a new designer he'd met in Milan. He was called Giorgio Armani.'

GFT manufactured the first Armani menswear collection and then quickly struck a manufacturing and distribution deal with the designer to make and sell his suits around the world. A new era in menswear began with the autumn 1976 collection, the first under the arrangement. The ascent of the designer name and the ascent of Italy as the centre of menswear design and manufacturing had begun.

'The first collection by Armani in 1975 was totally new, with new fabrics, new colours, new construction,' says Carlo, who was a company director at the time. 'It was innovative and shocking. People forget now that about 50 per cent of the styles didn't actually work well because the fabrics used were too soft and the jackets came apart, but it was so innovative people were forgiving.'

Armani's great innovation was to remove the internal padding and canvases from the suit, making it relaxed in shape and comfortable to wear. To sell the first Armani-GFT collection, Rivetti and Armani flew to the US in 1975. This was possibly the last time Signor Armani had to fly economy anywhere, as the business was a success from the start, having been picked up early by the Saks Fifth Avenue store group.

Although Pierre Cardin in France and Hardy Amies in the UK pioneered the licensing of their names as far back as the late 1950s, in the 1970s GFT became the masters of the designer licensing deal. Even before Armani, in 1974, GFT

> "... fashions in
> proud Italy,
> Whose manners
> still our tardy
> apish nation
> Limps after in
> base imitation."
>
> Duke of York, Act II,
> scene 1, *Richard II*
> William Shakespeare

had signed a contract with the French designer Emanuel Ungaro to produce his tailored womenswear. This in turn led to a menswear deal. Louis Féraud, another French designer, was another early menswear partner. The Roman couturier Valentino Garavani – known simply by his first name – was an important menswear catch in 1978. By the end of the 1980s, young American designers such as Joseph Abboud and Andrew Fezza had joined the club and in 1987 Calvin Klein signed a menswear deal with GFT, a move that greatly offended the Italian masters who disliked the American *arriviste* and felt he too readily copied their work.

By the mid-1980s, GFT was at the height of its power and influence. It made, sold and distributed around the world a large number of designer collections. While its expertise was in men's tailoring, it also made all types of men's garments and had an enviable womenswear business, too. By 1993 GFT had forty six companies worldwide, ran eighteen manufacturing plants globally and employed 10,000 people. It was one of the first European manufacturers to open a suit factory in China. But by then the company's

management had lost its grip on the business and it was acquired in 1994 by Gemina, one of the companies owned by the Agnelli family, which controlled Fiat. By the end of the decade, GFT had unravelled as a business, especially when Armani took back his licensing and production in 2000.

While establishing a whole new way of doing business at the upper level of the market – blazing a trail for the France-based luxury groups of the late 1980s and 1990s, such as Louis Vuitton-Moët Hennessy (LVMH) and Pinault-Printemps-Redoute (now called PPR) – GFT also led and encapsulated the remarkable growth of Italian men's fashion in the postwar period. Essential to the success of Italian menswear were four intrinsic factors: the skill of Italian fabric mills, the flair of its clothing designers, the readiness of its home market to embrace fashion change, and the Italians' skill in marketing abroad, especially in the US, the world's biggest consumer market.

The Rivetti family had been involved in cloth manufacturing in Biella, north of Milan, since the 1700s and its wool company Lanificio Rivetti had made a fortune producing fabrics for uniforms in the First World War. In 1925 they acquired the Turin-based company Donato Levi and Sons, which had been formed in 1887 as a ready-made clothing manufacturer. After the Second World War, three Rivetti brothers – Silvio, Pier Giorgio and Franco – decided to concentrate on making clothes rather than cloth. In 1949 Silvio had visited the US and had met the Ward family, which ran a sophisticated menswear manufacturer called Palm Beach Incorporated. He was introduced to a new concept that did not exist at that time in Italy – a scientific grading system for men's sizes that allowed a collection appropriate for mass manufacturing to be developed. Silvio brought the idea back to Italy and conducted an exhaustive survey of 40,000 Italians to build up an accurate database of the dimensions of men's bodies.

The initial attempt at a ready-made graded collection went badly wrong, as the formulae were based on the very different dimensions of the American males, but despite this hiccup, GFT began to build a reputation as possibly the most advanced mass suits manufacturer in the world. It industrialised the process to a new level. It brought an innovative, scientific and entrepreneurial approach that was very much in tune with the attitude of postwar Italy. In 1961 it opened the biggest factory in Italy, employing 400 people who made suits on a sophisticated, industrialised production line.

The company benefited in its home market from the massive migration of poor southern Italians to the industrial cities of the north. 'They didn't want to look like farm workers, so they had to buy a suit,' recalls Carlo Rivetti. 'In 1960 we opened a two-thousand-square-metre shop called Marus on Via Roma in Turin, selling our ready-made suits. For the next five years we would sell four thousand suits every Saturday. We also had a contract to make uniforms for the Italian railways, so we were able to keep a check on how Italian men's bodies were changing.'

GFT's main own label was Facis, a not very snappy acronym for Fabbrica Abiti Confezionati In Serie. When the company started exporting in the late 1960s, it soon found that Facis was not a name that many people outside Italy liked the sound of. By the time the first sales offices were opened in the UK and the US in 1971, the export brand had become SIDI, which was an acronym for Società Italiana Drapperie e Interni, an old Rivetti company name. GFT's fashion flair, its consistently reliable manufacturing quality and its prices, which offered excellent value for money rather than being cheap, made it an attractive business partner. It built a factory devoted solely to making suits for Marks & Spencer and had a significant business making own-label suits for stores such as Harrods.

Other Italian manufacturers aped GFT's success, such as Lubiam, founded by Luigi Bianchi in Mantova, which tied up with European socialite Egon von Furstenberg for its 'designer' offer, as well as having its own label and making suits for clients across Europe. By the time they added the glamour of the designer names in the mid-1970s, Italian manufacturers occupied a dominant place in the middle-to-upper sectors of the suits business.

As a precursor of the luxury market of today, in the decades after the Second World War Italian tailors had already established themselves as creative stylists for menswear, threatening the hegemony of Savile Row. Pre-eminent among these was Brioni, the company named after an Adriatic island that was a rich men's playground before the Second World War. In an example of putting a creative talent with a marketing talent, Brioni was formed in 1945 by Nazareno Fonticoli, a skilled tailor from Penne in the Abruzzi region, and Gaetano Savini, who was the business brain and salesman. Adjoining the Adriatic in east-central Italy, mountainous Abruzzi is the home of many of Italy's top tailors, including Caraceni, Ciro Giuliano and Del Rosso. Menswear legend has it that the local expertise was honed in the late nineteenth and early twentieth centuries when the celebrated musician Francesco Paolo Tosti, who was singing master to the British royal family and was knighted by Edward VII, sent his Savile Row suits back for relations to wear, where local tailors unpicked them to discover how they were constructed.

In 1945 the Brioni pair opened their own boutique, offering a made-to-measure service, on Via Barberini in Rome, the main tourist destination of Italy. Key to Brioni's international reputation was the wooing of the American elite. The pair met Giovanbattista Giorgini, the aristocrat who was one of the founding fathers of Italian high fashion. In 1951 he organised the first Italian womenswear high fashion show in

Above: The young tailor Enrico Isaia created the high-class Italian producer Isaia that is part of Classico Italia, the exclusive group of menswear producers today.

288 presentations, almost one every month. This was, as Brioni's biographer Farid Chenoune has written, 'a feat which took the flair of a visionary and the persistence of a promoter to accomplish at a time when there was nothing else of the kind in the "no man's land" of men's fashion'.[1]

Riding alongside the rise of Italian high-class womenswear and the growing influence of Italian cinema, Brioni's flamboyance and extravagance was lauded by the press and attracted the patronage of the all-important American movie stars. The Brioni archives include photos of Henry Fonda, Victor Mature, Clark Gable, John Wayne, Rock Hudson and Gary Cooper being measured for suits. Brioni's new look meant it could be hailed as 'Dior for men' in *Life* magazine in October 1955.

In 1960 the company introduced the wording 'Brioni Roman Style' on its label and began to combine made-to-measure with mass production in a purpose-built factory in Penne. There in 1980 it introduced its own tailoring school to ensure that the skills of cutting and sewing are perpetuated. Students at the Scuola Superiore di Sartoria have to complete a four-year course before they are fully qualified tailors. As Chenoune observed: '... the production of a made-to-order suit entails more than 150 steps, requiring eighteen to thirty hours of work, with roughly half this time spent in hand crafting: preparation, tacking, stitching, finishing, from cutting the fabric for each client to hand-sewing buttonholes, the whole process interspersed with more than forty pressings.'

Brioni's global profile was raised even higher when it won the rights to dress that international figure of style, James Bond, from *GoldenEye* (1995) to *Casino Royale* (2006). (Tom Ford took over dressing Bond in 2008's *Quantum of Solace;* the Tom Ford suits are made in Italy by Ermenegildo Zegna.) As the Bond movies portrayed, despite the outrageous styles of its early days, Brioni is best known

Florence for journalists and buyers from the US. The following year Brioni was invited exclusively to dress the men who escorted the female models in the presentation. This led to Brioni's lavish and colourful evening wear and smoking jackets, such as one in bright-red shantung silk, being displayed in the windows of B Altman & Co, the celebrated department store on Fifth Avenue. Brioni had arrived in the US.

In 1952, this time on its own, Brioni presented its collection in the elegant setting of the Sala Bianca in the Pitti Palace in Florence in what is considered to be the first major fashion show dedicated solely to menswear. It was a momentous turning point in the presentation of menswear and ultimately led to the now biannual ritual of men's catwalk shows in Milan and Paris.

Savini and Fonticoli had uncovered the power of live presentation. In 1954 they held their first show in New York. Between 1952 and 1977 the company made an astonishing now for a refined, discreet approach that appeals to an international audience of well-heeled jet-setters that can afford its very high prices. In the words of Chenoune: 'All that remains of that original "vulgarity" is a faint accent, an offhand touch, a kind of studied *sprezzatura* or "nonchalance", as they like to call it on the Via Barberini.'[2]

That Italian attitude to menswear was hugely instrumental in creating the concept of men's fashion as we understand it today. Italian men like the notion known as *fare figura,* or to cut a figure, to keep up appearances, especially when making a *passegiata,* a stroll around town.

Throughout the 1950s the Italians brought a fresh attitude to menswear that targeted the young consumer. As writer Colin McDowell observed:

> *Italian tailors knew how to cut clothes to flatter, but then so did Savile Row and Ivy League tailors. What made Italian style different was its point of view. Turning their backs on accepted line, Italian tailors set out to create clothes which not only looked young but, unlike the products of traditional tailoring, only looked good on the young. They were not adapting an existing line to younger men's taste, but, much more radically, were treating young men as a completely new market. This was a fresh concept in the staid and traditional world of gentlemen's tailoring and its effect was to bring youthful fashion into the mainstream.*[3]

The now-classic Italian look of the late 1950s and early 1960s was a short 'bum-freezer' jacket, high-closing narrow lapels and narrow, sleek trousers that demanded a suitably narrow winkle-picker shoe. This style inspired the Continental look in the US in the late 1950s and the British Mods in the early 1960s.

By 1959 *Men's Wear* was giving its readers an 'Italian Style Forecast'. 'The current Italian style is towards a more virile and casual look, according to Angelo Litrico, the Rome tailor,' readers of the issue of 17 January 1959 learned. An early adopter of Italian fashions in London was Cecil Gee, an influential menswear retailer who had a shop in Shaftesbury Avenue in London's theatre district. He had made his reputation bringing over directional styles from the US in the postwar period before he moved on to Italian style.

Like *Richard II's* Duke of York, the reaction of the London menswear establishment and many conventional British men to the revolutionary Italian styles was defensive and critical. In February 1959, the influential BBC news programme *Panorama* examined the Italian men's fashion phenomenon. Cecil Gee expressed his displeasure at the jingoistic bias of the film in a letter to *Men's Wear* on 21 February:

> *The interviews might give the public the impression that only eccentric types of men were interested in Italian style clothes. This, of course, is quite incorrect. We have had phenomenal success in our own store with Italian clothes, selling to all ages, and even to men of normal conservative taste. The BBC spent almost a day in our Shaftesbury Avenue store, where they interviewed well-dressed customers who gave their own opinions of the Italian trend in men's fashions. But in the actual programme other interviews, undoubtedly taken in small suburban shops, were merged into the same film. This would give an entirely wrong interpretation of the average customer's opinion.*

Right: A flamboyant ensemble from Brioni's 1969 'Sinfonia Blu' collection. There are more ideas in the waistcoat than in an entire wardrobe of conventional suits.

Above: From the mid-1970s to the late '90s GFT was the global leader in making and marketing high-quality tailoring to the middle and upper-middle segment, cementing Italy's reputation as the factory for men's styles. This image is from 1985.

Left: By 1975 Italian designers like Carlo Palazzi were setting the international pace with their body-conscious suits which displayed wide lapels and wider flares.

Gee was supported in his view by one Mr F Yates, the deputy merchandise controller for men's and boys' wear at the Nottingham Co-operative Society, a mainstream retailer in the Midlands, far away from the bright lights of London. He wrote to the BBC, with a copy to *Men's Wear*, to complain: 'As a retailer who has already sold hundreds of these garments, I consider they are very elegant and not at all grotesque. I do hope that in the future when you are dealing with menswear you will treat them with much more respect.'

Such resistance to Italian menswear now seems strange to anyone who has witnessed the rise of designer names in the past two decades. Designers as diverse as Gianni Versace, Romeo Gigli, and Domenico Dolce and Stefano Gabbana each had a distinct 'handwriting', but somehow always exhibited some aspect of Italian bravura and love of fine

fabrics. The two fashion brands most impressively reinvented during the past twenty years – Prada and Gucci – have reaffirmed Italy's pole position for directional menswear. Apart from the different styling, the world's men can thank the Italians for their expertise in developing new, lighter, but high-performance cloths for men's suits. The mills around Biella deal with the top-end qualities, while the district of Prato, just north of Florence, is known for its more commercial production. Italian companies such as Cerruti and Ermenegildo Zegna were pioneers of the vertical approach that saw them making the cloths and then using them to make suits under their own name.

Italian fabric is world-renowned for its quality, adding to the country's menswear credentials. By the mid-1970s, as we have seen, the power of Italian menswear, led by its suit production, was in the ascendant. In 1971 leading Italian manufacturers began showing to international buyers twice a year in Florence at the Pitti Uomo exhibition. More than thirty years on, it is the pre-eminent gathering of the world's menswear buyers, who examine the collections of upmarket tailoring specialists such as Pal Zileri, Tombolini, Lubiam, Cantarelli, Corneliani and Hilton. Also using Pitti Uomo as their twice-yearly showcase are the members of the Classico Italia association, which represents a select group of luxury artisanal tailoring producers such as d'Avenza, Santandrea, Kiton, Isaia and Belvest. These super-expensive producers keep alive Italy's reputation for exquisite hand-tailoring. As always, the US is a major market for these firms.

The bi-annual Milan menswear catwalk shows, held straight after Pitti Uomo in January and June, generally attract the globally bigger brands – Armani, Prada, Gucci, Versace – than the rival event in Paris, attesting to Italy's hold on the menswear market. The twice-yearly trips to Florence and Milan remind international menswear observers just how well-dressed Italian men are.

"It is sometimes said that the French spend their money on their food, the English on their gardens, and the Italian on their clothes."

Hardy Amies,

An ABC of Men's Fashion

Right: Having revived the fortunes of first Gucci and then YSL, the American Tom Ford now has his own stylish luxury line, Tom Ford Menswear, which is manufactured by the Ermenegildo Zegna group in Italy.

Opposite: From the late 1970s Giorgio Armani redefined how a man's suit could look and feel by removing much of the traditional inner structure. Here, in 1983, the red tie adds a rare burst of colour to his own outfit.

Left: In 1974, the always immaculate Valentino shows he knows all about the little details, such as just two cuff buttons on a one-button SB.

Overleaf: This overtly gay imagery from Dolce & Gabbana in 2004 was aimed at men who had well-toned bodies to carry off the slimline suits.

ABBANA

Right: In 1960, in Federico Fellini's *La Dolce Vita,* Marcello Mastroianni showed an elegance that came to epitomise Italian style.

Opposite: The slim lines, spare details and neutral colours of Prada's suits were hugely influential when they appeared in the mid-1990s. This version is from the Autumn/Winter 2003 collection.

The checked suit

A checked fabric requires particular expertise to weave, considerable skill to tailor and a good deal of confidence to wear well. But it gives a man a chance to express his personality while wearing even a conventionally cut suit, or the excuse to make a dramatic impression.

Far left: These three-piece versions from the British multiple tailor Hector Powe in 1964 are striking enough to require only plain shirts and unpatterned ties.

Centre left: A brown glen check suit projects the quiet confidence of a man who has 'arrived' in this mid-1960s ad for Hickey Freeman of the US.

Centre right: A bold check can also provide 3-D 'surface interest' in a complicated weave such as this one, from an unidentified French label in 1970.

Far right: In 1973 Rod Stewart goes for the dandy look in a neat shepherd's check that appears to have been selected to complement the highlights in his hair.

chapter FIVE *US Male*

> ## "Americans were about as well prepared for the Peacock Revolution as they had been for Pearl Harbor."
>
> *Esquire* magazine

America has exported to the world Levi's, Lycra and the Hawaiian shirt worn outside the trousers, but it has tended to import its styling for men's suits. Throughout the twentieth century, and certainly after the old order collapsed in Europe after 1918, the United States has been the biggest consumer market and the most powerful nation on earth. But, as befits a country that was created by immigrants, it has been open to ideas from elsewhere, while always being ready to subvert what it borrowed to present a fresh, modern and sometimes brash approach. This analysis certainly applies to men's suits.

The US always presents a mass of contradictions. Despite the entrepreneurial spirit that built the country, in men's formal fashion, America has been surprisingly conservative, for many decades taking its lead from the prevailing mores of the WASP (White Anglo-Saxon Protestant) ruling class of the original northeastern states.

Until the late 1980s or early 1990s, a suit was the generally expected business attire of the American male. The term 'white-collar worker', denoting an office employee who wore a suit, shirt and tie, was coined by novelist Upton Sinclair in 1919. The somewhat stifling conformity of the US business community was most famously highlighted in *The Man In The Gray Flannel Suit,* a 1955 novel by Sloan Wilson. It was

made into a movie in 1956 with Gregory Peck in the title role of disenchanted businessman Tom Rath and stimulated debate about the stodginess that characterised the American white-collar community.

In their seminal work, Esquire's *Encyclopaedia of 20th Century Men's Fashions,* O E Schoeffler and William Gale wittily observed about the explosion of creativity in mid-1960s menswear from Europe: 'Americans were about as well prepared for the Peacock Revolution as they had been for Pearl Harbor.' And it was not until 1964 that the US found its first local menswear designer, John Weitz, who, like his counterparts in Europe, had made his reputation in womenswear.

While its business uniform of the masculine white-collar workforce may have been unexciting and slow moving, the US gave the world the other extreme of the style spectrum – it dressed the stars of the biggest showbiz industry in the world, encompassing first music, then movies and later television. This cultural stream proved to be far more interesting to historians of the suit, as did the influence from the often segregated Afro-American and Latino citizens. As in other countries, in the past fifty years or more one has had to look beyond the ruling elites of the US to find the creative forces in men's style.

Appropriately for a nation with one of the largest populations in the world, America was a pioneer in the mass industrialisation of clothing production. As early as 6 September 1902, reviewing the situation in the US, the British trade magazine *Men's Wear* warned its traditionalist, tailoring-focused readers of the dangers of 'A 'Ready-Mades' Invasion'. Its editorial commented:

> *A visit to America cannot fail to impress the stranger with the relative importance of*

the ready-made clothing industry there. Men of far higher position and greater wealth wear ready-made clothes (and this is true even in cities like New York and Philadelphia) than in this country. It seems ludicrous to say so, but there is a considerable and respected trade in ready-made dress suits – not for waiters, but for people who dress for dinner when they dine out and go to the theatre . . . There is no doubt to the reason for this. Richer men buy ready-made clothes in America rather than in England, because the ready-made clothing itself in America is better than in England. The best materials are not thought too good for making up into ready-made clothes in the United States. The best workmanship is not thought too good. And these suits are made in very finely graded sizes and fittings. It is perfectly practicable, in an emergency, to buy a ready-made overcoat, in America, and not look in the least conspicuous as a result of this transaction. Outside of the big cities practically everyone wears ready-made stuff in America, and a good many unsuspected people do so inside these cities.

The British writer's incredulity that men of 'higher position and greater wealth' should buy off-the-peg is clear. But the demands for uniforms for the American Civil War in the 1860s had contributed to the mechanisation of the process of making clothes. The flood of immigration in the post-Civil War period was another spur – a ready market needed ready-made clothes.

As in Europe, the period of actually making clothes in the US has been short. The Americans were among the first to go looking for lower-cost supply bases among their near neighbours of Mexico, Latin America and the Caribbean, as well as the even more productive Far East. Today few suit manufacturers still have factories in the fifty states, but the ones that do can claim a long heritage.

The most famous American suit name internationally is Brooks Brothers, a business that managed to dress the upper classes and those that aspired to join them for both work and play. Its own official history describes it as 'the single greatest influence on men's fashion in America'. The first store was opened at 116 Cherry Street in Lower Manhattan, New York City, on 7 April 1818 by Henry Sands Brooks, a forty-six-year-old provisioner who had previously supplied goods to seafarers, trappers and similarly adventurous entrepreneurs. Henry's sons Daniel, John, Elisha and Edward joined the business and, in 1850, seventeen years after their father's death, they renamed the family firm Brooks Brothers.

Between 1818 and 1850 the population of New York soared from 125,000 to 630,000 and the city itself developed from a busy, if rough, seaport to a more significant commercial and cultural centre. It is generally accepted that Brooks Brothers was among the first concerns to offer ready-made clothing – it was certainly advertising the fact by the time of the 1849 California gold rush; a report at the time revealed that the company had 1,500 people making its clothes.

Henry Sands Brooks' statement of intent from 1818 guided his firm's attitude. The aim was: 'To make and deal only in merchandise of the best quality, to sell it at a fair profit only, and to deal with people who seek and are capable of appreciating such merchandise.' Alongside the ready-mades, Brooks Brothers also provided custom or bespoke tailoring for its higher-class clientele. As London was the home of correct tailoring, Brooks Brothers predictably looked to the UK for the proper raw materials, namely fine woollens and worsteds from English and Scottish mills.

The earliest and most famous innovation of Brooks' tailoring was the Number One sack suit. Originally with a four-button jacket in 1900, and a three-button version from 1918, the cut was identified by its unpadded 'natural' shoulders that sloped easily from the neck, modest notched lapels, relatively soft jacket construction, a centre back vent and straight-leg trousers. This quintessential Brooks Brothers suit has barely changed over the past hundred years.

New York City was the centre of the US's clothing industry and many immigrants from Europe brought with them skills that found favour with firms such as Brooks Brothers. Proximity to the fabric mills of New England was an important factor in the efficiency of the industry. In 1899, in Rochester, upstate New York (a thriving centre of men's clothing production), Jeremiah Hickey teamed up with Jacob Freeman and a couple of associates to form a manufacturing business. Within a year, the business was called Hickey & Freeman Co, by 1908 it was Hickey Freeman and today it remains as the only suit manufacturer now operating in Rochester. It was expensive in its early days and it is expensive today. In contrast to many of its illustrious competitors, Hickey Freeman never advertised its products nationally, but relied on word of mouth and recommendation, rather like a traditional bespoke tailor. The company did, however, have the foresight – and the demand – to justify opening a three-storey, 77,000-square-foot factory in 1912. The usual system in those days was for different tailors to work on different parts of ready-made suits in different locations – often their own homes were

their workshops. The component parts were only brought together for finishing and shipping, so Hickey Freeman's single factory approach was innovative. In the factory, an assembly-line system brought a new efficiency and level of quality. 'Keep The Quality Up' was adopted as Hickey Freeman's company motto. Over the decades, the business has maintained a high level of handwork in its products.

In 1964 Hickey Freeman became a subsidiary of another grand old name of US tailoring, Hart Schaffner & Marx (now Hartmarx Corporation). Founded in 1887 in Chicago, it was the product of the alliance between brothers Max and Harry Hart and their distant cousin Joseph Schaffner. Marcus Marx was another relative who invested in the business, but had nothing to do with its running. Schaffner is regarded as the architect of the firm's success; in 1897 he used $5,000 to launch what was possibly the first men's clothing advertising campaign. Probably the most famous stunt occurred in 1918 when the company advertised widely in France with a message for the thousands of soon-to-be-home American soldiers – 'Stylish clothes are ready for you in the good old US of A – all-wool guaranteed – Hart Schaffner & Marx'.

The company can claim some other firsts. In 1900 it was the first US manufacturer to boast that it only used 'all wool' fabrics, as opposed to cheaper blends. In 1906 HSM was the first to produce proportioned suits with basic body types, offering tall, short, stout and thin models. It abolished contract homeworkers – tailors and seamstresses who worked outside the factory on piecework – in 1910 and agreed a collective bargaining agreement with the powerful garment workers' union in 1911. It guaranteed colour-fastness as early as 1915. Its first zipper went to its trousers in 1936. Shortly after the Second World War, as the mass migration from city centres began, it opened a store in one of the first suburban shopping malls. In 1951 the company produced its first suit in a fabric blended from wool and Du Pont's polyester brand Dacron.

Another name that is approaching its centenary is Oxxford, which was established in Chicago in 1916 by Jacob and Lewis Weinberg. The brand offers custom tailoring and made-to-measure, but is best known for its traditionally styled ready-made garments. It stresses the very high level of handwork in its production, with something like forty-five pressings during manufacture and an estimated 5,500 hand stitches in each suit. Oxxford's patrons have included Cary Grant, President Johnson and Al Capone.

A characteristic of the American menswear business has been its readiness to embrace new fabric and fibre developments. Given the country's wide range of temperatures, there was always a call for 'tropical' fabrics such as cotton, linen and seersucker, and in the 1930s the US readily accepted tropical worsteds that weighed as little as 8.5oz or 9oz to the yard, a drop from the previously common 10.5oz or 12oz (suitings of 18oz and 20oz were not uncommon in the UK at the time). As early as the mid-1920s, suits made of rayon, an artificial silk, were on offer and by the late 1940s fabrics blending wool and nylon began to be used, as, though less likely to 'breathe', they were more resistant to wearing out.

The early 1950s were the high point – or low point, depending on your point of view – of the development of synthetic fibres. In 1951 the first commercially available suits made from Dacron, Du Pont's polyester fibre, appeared. The chemical company also aggressively marketed its Orlon brand of acrylic, which was a substitute for wool; the luxurious Brioni of Italy was persuaded to style trend predictions for Orlon. In the interest of comfort, polyester was knitted into a softly draping fabric for suits in the 1960s and 1970s. For the suit purists, this is when America lost its way and its taste.

Historically, extreme suits have provoked extreme reactions in the US, most notoriously in the so-called 'zoot suit riots' of 1943. According to a now-discredited legend, the first zoot suit was ordered in Gainesville, Georgia, in 1939 by a busboy called Clyde Duncan who wanted to look like Rhett Butler in *Gone With The Wind*. The zoot suit was all about exaggerated proportions – massively wide padded shoulders, huge peaked lapels, a fitted waist on a long, long jacket that draped to the knees, with trousers that were fitted way above the natural waistline, billowing from waist pleats in a baggy silhouette that ended with very narrow, cuffed ankles. The black entertainer Cab Calloway wore a polished version in the 1943 film *Stormy Weather,* but on the streets the zoot suit was the uniform of an admittedly small number of flamboyant young blacks and Latinos.

The zoot suit infringed the USA's War Production Board's rationing of fabric – which banned even turn-ups on conventional suits – and some citizens viewed the wearing of the outfits as un-American. In June 1943, ugly fights broke out in Los Angeles between off-duty servicemen and zoot-suited Latino youths; similar cultural confrontations were witnessed in other cities. This would not be the last time that the apparent stylistic excesses of the black and Latino communities offended Middle America.

Up until the early 1950s the traditions of London tailoring were probably the main source of reference for US suits, but ten years after the war, the influence of Italy began to overtake Savile Row, with millions of Americans of Italian heritage forming an enthusiastic market. As early as 1950, the style magazine *Esquire* had introduced Mr T, a new trim look for suits that narrowed the shoulders by an inch and slimmed the lapels down by three-quarters of an inch. The well-heeled collegians who attended the Ivy League schools of the northeast states – Brown, Columbia, Cornell, Dartmouth, Harvard, University of Pennsylvania, Princeton

and Yale – were already going for a neat, narrow look. This Ivy League style was essentially the pared-down, no-nonsense approach of a Brooks Brothers Number One sack suit.

The country was ready in 1956 for the Continental suit, which was a modification of the Italian look of the day. More body-conscious than anything from England or Brooks Brothers, the jacket was shorter than before, had narrow, sleek shoulders and a notably nipped-in waist, all complemented by slimmer trousers. Variations of the Continental were fashionable into the mid-1960s. Having won favour with stylish musicians such as Miles Davis and the Motown stable of male vocal groups, the look was re-exported to Europe where it influenced the Mod wardrobe.

Although American suit traditionalists continued to look to Savile Row for inspiration, newer European names were courted in the early 1960s by American retailers and manufacturers who wanted to inject fashion into their ranges. In 1962 Pierre Cardin's styles were bought by Bonwit Teller, the department-store group, while in 1966 England's Hardy Amies signed a lucrative deal to act as a design consultant to Genesco, at the time one of the biggest clothing groups in the US.

Another important aspect of American menswear is its relatively early adoption of men's style magazines. *Apparel Arts* was a trade quarterly that first appeared in 1931. This inspired, in autumn 1933, the publication of *Esquire* as a consumer magazine. Originally conceived as a quarterly, it went monthly after its first edition. In 1958 *Esquire* launched a spin-off called *Gentleman's Quarterly*, which over the years has been developed – under different owners – into the magazine now known universally as *GQ*.

According to its own encyclopaedia, the *Esquire* publishers had a clear image of their target market back in the 1930s:

Above: Sean John Combs, a.k.a. Puff Daddy and P Diddy, began his career wearing urban streetwear. Now he is usually seen in a finely tailored suit, the uniform of success, as seen here at the Monaco Grand Prix in 2001.

'We constantly had a beau ideal in mind; the man of taste, with a sense of style and a respect for quality.' Although the circulation of *Esquire* and subsequent titles was small, their influence among the taste makers and the menswear industry has, at times, been considerable. In 1968 *Esquire* sponsored the first International Designers Conference, where the conventionally tailored suit was threatened by the velvet Edwardian jacket, the safari suit, the Nehru suit, the waistcoat suit and the knitted suit.

In the past three decades, America has ridden a number of socio-fashion trends that have produced their own short-lived suit fads. Although American casualwear and the general relaxation of social rules of dress have spread around the world, suit 'exports' have been few. It's been fun to observe, via the media of film, television and, lately, music videos such stylistic adventures as *Saturday Night Fever*-style three-piece disco suits, *Miami Vice* relaxed

Above: Barack Obama has made a rather safe two-button navy blue suit from Hart Schaffner Marx his presidential uniform. The company is based in Obama's adopted home town of Chicago.

Right: Harry S Truman, who for a short time ran a haberdashery business in Kansas City, Missouri, was the thirty-third president of the USA (1945–53) and possibly the best dressed. He certainly showed an interest in clothes and an individual style that most of his modern successors have lacked.

styling, 1980s power dressing, and the spare, black, anonymous suits of *Reservoir Dogs* and *Pulp Fiction*, not to mention rappers swapping tracksuits for bespoke suits once they made it big.

Americans have been excellent in marketing designer names – Ralph Lauren, Calvin Klein, Joseph Abboud – but few of their major successes outside their home territory have been in suits, unless they have stayed close, like Lauren, to British tradition.

The concept of dress-down Friday and 'business casual' – in which employees are positively encouraged to ditch the suit – is an American invention that horrifies suit traditionalists. While suit sales continue to decline generally in the US, it is also the country that supplies most of the clients for Savile Row – about forty per cent of the Row's entire business is with Americans and some tailoring firms rely even more on

transatlantic customers. It is still the consumer market that most aspirational suit brands in Europe would like to crack. And it is the country that is most likely to have small numbers of knowledgeable and enthusiastic men reading books on how to dress well by style writers Alan Flusser or Nicholas Antongiavanni, or swapping esoteric notes and queries on websites such as askandyaboutclothes.com.

Antongiavanni in particular bewails current levels of taste in the US. In his entertaining and informative book, *The Suit*, he writes:

> *Making things worse [for men in America] is the difficulty of finding decent clothes to buy even if you know what looks good. There used to be two or three bespoke tailors of repute in every American city larger than a hamlet, and dozens in each of the great metropolises. But today only New York is served by more than two, and few other cities can claim even one. And the great college towns, those erstwhile breeding grounds of style which used to support legions of delightful haberdasheries, now could not sustain even a mail-order business. This is [because] American tastes having declined precipitously, there is no longer sufficient demand to maintain all those shops and tailors.*
>
> *Good off-the-peg clothing can still be found, but its purveyors are few. The stuff that is readily available everywhere is not good, because when mass marketing anything it always pays to appeal to the lowest common denominator, and in our time that is low indeed. In addition, the cost to make quality garments has risen while the cost of most everything else has declined.[1]*

Left: The boys are back in town: Dean Martin and Frank Sinatra bring a taste of American swagger to the UK as they land at Heathrow in August 1961. Hollywood tailor Sy Devore may well have been their stylist.

Above: Roger Sterling (played by John Slattery) and Don Draper (Jon Hamm) represent traditional and modern menswear from the early 1960s in the award-winning TV series *Mad Men*, which was first aired in 2007 and set in the Sterling Cooper ad agency on Madison Avenue. Costume designer Janie Bryant uses authentic 1960s styles for all the outfits.

Right: Dressed to impress, a zoot-suited night owl checks out the action at the Savoy ballroom in Harlem in the late 1930s.

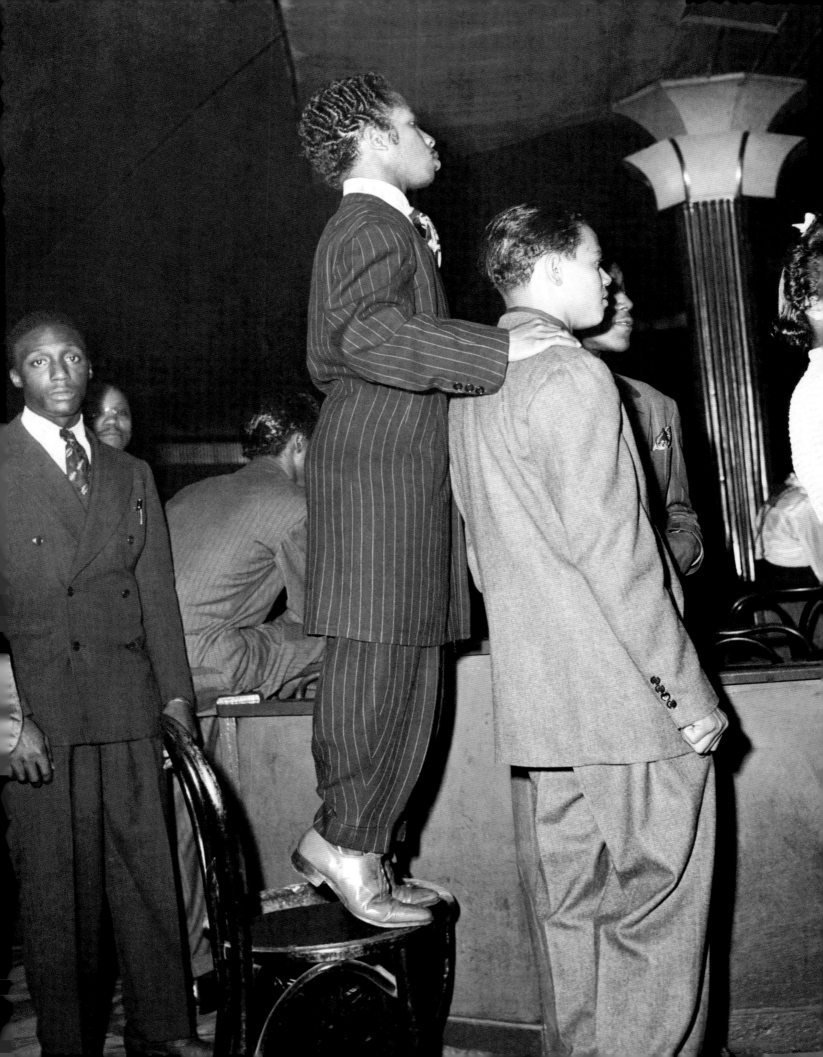

Left and above: Style never goes out of style. In 1987, Calvin Klein, a designer who made his name with modern sportswear, goes for a classic wide-lapelled DB in a grey chalkstripe fabic, reflecting almost exactly the choice made forty years earlier by a beaming Frank Sinatra in the late 1940s.

Above: Establishment dress: Robert, Edward and John Kennedy wearing classic American sack suits in the mid-1950s. It is generally accepted that John at least had many suits made in the American style on Savile Row.

Right: Taking his major reference points from classic British tailoring, in a forty-year career Ralph Lauren has always championed relaxed elegance in his tailoring. He's seen here with his dog Rugby in 1998.

> "*I always wear a suit — looking one's best is good for confidence ... Dressing well is also a sign of respect, for your-self and others.*"
>
> Donald Trump

Right: Start 'em young: there's a fine selection of style options in this line-up of young suit wearers in Harlem on Easter Sunday 1982. These days, few cultures dress boys as young as these in tailored suits.

The white suit

In the days before dry cleaning and fabric protectors such as Scotchguard, wearing a white suit was an indication of wealth. 'If this becomes dirty,' the wearer seemed to say, 'I have people to clean it for me, and other suits to wear'. It was also a symbol of gentility, an artistic streak, or a dandified attitude to dress. And it was cooler to wear in hot, sunny climes. Today modern, dirt-resistant fabrics have made white suits a more practical option, but they are still unusual enough to attract attention.

Far left: In the TV series of 1971 and 1972, the dandy adventurer *Jason King* (played by Peter Wyngarde) looked totally at home in a white suit.

Centre left: This elegant fashion plate is actor Sydney Barraclough in or about 1910. He worked in London and New York, but this is more likely to have been an American suit. Note the breast pockets on both sides of the jacket.

Centre right: Samuel Langhorne Clemens, a.k.a. Mark Twain, took to wearing white suits only in his late sixties. He died in 1910, aged seventy-four.

Far right: Tony Montana (Al Pacino) goes for gangster chic as *Scarface* (1983).

chapter SIX
Passion From Paris

The British trade weekly *Men's Wear* had international news for its readers on 28 July 1962:

> *The most quiet and deft of revolutions in the man's fashion is now taking place. The French believe they are taking over. Ever since the Italian Look withered last year, international men's clothes have needed a strong lead. That lead now seems to be coming from Paris, from the top names in women's haute couture. The couturiers who lent their names to ties and handkerchiefs are starting to put in men's boutiques. And those who already have boutiques are moving into mass production in the garment industry. All the big names – Dior, Balmain, Lanvin, Cardin, de Givenchy and so on – are rapidly expanding into the man's fashion industry: and exporting.*

This was not the first time that England and France had jousted on the subject of men's style. In June 1520 near Calais, on the Field of the Cloth of Gold, Henry VIII met Francis I for a summit meeting that turned out to be something of a fashion contest between the two nations and their rulers. Two hundred and fifty years later, Anglomania was the term applied to a French fad for the relative simplicity of London's men's fashions. And in the middle of the nineteenth century, the Comte Alfred d'Orsay was hailed on both sides of the channel as the supremo in all matters of taste and fashion, and the only natural successor to George 'Beau' Brummell, despite the fact that d'Orsay favoured colourful opulence where the Beau preached restraint.

Savile Row had attracted plenty of celebrated French patrons throughout the nineteenth century – the leading English tailoring firm Henry Poole justified opening a branch in Paris in 1904 and closed only when the Germans invaded in 1940 – and, as early as 1903, during the period of the Entente Cordiale, *Men's Wear* was reporting on the latest trends from Paris, *La Ville Lumière*.

Internationally, elegant performers such as Maurice Chevalier, Charles Boyer, Charles Aznavour and Sacha Distel bridged the generations on both sides of the Second World War, reminding the world of the style of the French suit wearer.

The British alarm call of 1962, however, heralded new developments that were to change the face of menswear – the rise of the designer name, the eclipse of the traditional tailor, the replacement of tradition by fashion and the rise of the adolescent market.

Central to the establishment of Paris as the menswear capital of fashion was Pierre Cardin. Born on 7 July 1922, he had been apprenticed to Manby, a clothier in Vichy, when he was fourteen. Moving to Paris, he worked for the leading womenswear couturiers Paquin, Schiaparelli and Christian Dior before setting up his own business in 1950. A far-sighted innovator, he opened a women's boutique called Eve in 1954 and three years later added a male equivalent, Adam, which sold accessories and small items.

His first menswear collection – showing what became known as his 'cylinder' look – was unveiled at the Crillon Hotel in Paris in 1960, using students as models, which

Previous page: French pop singer Jacques Dutronc looks totally at home in a Renoma-style suit in about 1967. Those are impressively parallel trousers.

Right: The nowadays underestimated Pierre Cardin, photographed in 1960 in a suit probably made for him by Gilbert Féruch. The collarless jacket was later adopted by The Beatles for a short period. Cardin was *the* most influential menswear designer until Giorgio Armani arrived in the mid-1970s.

itself was newsworthy. The collection included suits with the collarless, lapel-less jackets that were soon to be come known as 'Beatle' jackets, but more important was the line and cut of the suit. Rather than being padded or shaped to enhance the wearer's body, the jackets simply followed the natural body shape while the trousers hugged the hips in harmony.

In 1971, English writer Nik Cohn positively enthused about Cardin's lasting influence:

> *Just this one perception, that clothes should not contradict the body beneath them, was enough to change the whole conception of what suits were about, and all the styles of the last decade – single-breasted, double-breasted, safari, Nehru or whatever – have followed the same basic principles. It is as simple as this: if you are wearing a suit as you read this and it has anything to do with fashion, its label is irrelevant. In essence you must be wearing the Cardin jacket.[1]*

Colin McDowell is equally impressed with Cardin's vision:

> *Fashion history not been kind to Cardin. It has denied him enormous credit for expanding the parameters of masculine dress. He is arguably the most influential menswear designer of the twentieth century in that, like Hardy Amies, he changed attitudes to dress in men who had relatively little interest in their appearance and who would never have dreamed of walking through the doors of a boutique. He took the traditional pared-down silhouette of British tailoring and gave it a classless, timeless quality on which designers have built ever since ... His*

strength was to make function his chief focus. Attractive details on his clothes are pleasing because they have a purpose.[2]

The couturier Christian Dior had lent his name to a men's tie collection in 1950 and another couturier, Jacques Fath, had followed his example, but Cardin became the expert at licensing his name, selling the rights for a manufacturer to make products that carried his name. In 1961 Bril, one of the leading French garment manufacturers of the day, brought out the first complete line of men's ready-to-wear signed by Pierre Cardin. As French costume historian Farid Chenoune has pointed out, it is difficult to estimate how quickly Cardin's styles began to be commercially significant; he estimates that it took three years for the phenomenon to make a mark on sales in the shops.[3]

The space-age designs from Cardin that are often featured as amusing reminders of early 1960s excess were never commercially important and were probably not intended to be. But they did remind people of where Cardin's vision was. 'The past is not interesting to me,' he told English writer Rodney Bennett-England.[4]

'At a time when people from all walks of life mingle on the street, at work, on the beach, or at ski resorts, fashion design can no longer be restricted to an elite,' Cardin said in another interview in 1965. 'My goal is to present design at the service of an increasingly wide public.'[5]

While this egalitarian sentiment may be admirable, Cardin's long-term reputation has suffered because he was astonishingly promiscuous in granting licences across the world. By the early 1980s Cardin had 800 or more licensees making all manner of products in nearly 100 countries, but many of them went for a very low common denominator, which betrayed their intellectual origins.

Cardin sold to the American department-store group Bonwit Teller in 1962 and the Cardin look and the man's reputation was boosted in 1963 when The Beatles wore Cardin-style suits made for them by London showbiz tailor Dougie Millings, who added a few touches such as braiding. The collarless style, although it echoed the look of a traditional Tyrolean jacket, was inspired by the suits Cardin had made for himself by Gilbert Féruch, another French *createur* who today does not receive the recognition he probably deserves.

Born in Algeria in 1924, Féruch opened a tailor's shop in Paris that attracted artistic clients like Cardin, Yves St Laurent and Pablo Picasso. If he is remembered at all today, Féruch is celebrated as the first Westerner to try out the stand-up Nehru collar. He first used it on a tuxedo for mime master Marcel Marceau. It hit its fashion heights in about 1968.

Like Cardin, Féruch wanted to simplify men's suits, to have longer, slimmer jackets with less interfacing. By 1962 Féruch was showing suit jackets with narrow shoulders and deep vents – it was to become a recognisably French look.

Féruch became a consultant to Cecil Gee, the London menswear store that had been championing foreign fashion looks since just after the Second World War. After his first London show in 1965, Cardin earned a similar contract with Associated Tailors, which owned the multiple chains John Temple and Neville Reed. The company opened Pierre Cardin shops in the Strand in London in September 1966 and in the prosperous Cheshire town of Wilmslow in 1967. It is not recorded how they fared, but menswear retailers in the UK complained that French-made suits did not sell well because their cut was much too narrow for solid-bodied Britons.

Another important cross-channel influence was the exchange of stylistic ideas between teenage music fans. In the words of Chenoune, by the mid-1960s the fashion trade in France, as in the UK, 'began courting the new princes of consumption, middle-class adolescents'.[6] In 1962, Le Drugstore, a café boutique on Champs-Elysées, became the gathering point for an initially small group of well-to-do high school or college kids. They favoured a quasi-English style of suit, with fitted waist and narrow shoulders. Grey or brown flannel or navy-blue serge were the preferred fabrics. Blazers, houndstooth sports jackets with two vents, mohair or cashmere sweaters, and club ties were all part of the look, which merged the English and the US Ivy League styles.

These youngsters went to Marina, an old tailor on Rue Vernier in the seventeenth arrondisement, who was the first to cut flat-fronted, wide-bottomed trousers with small cuffs known as *marinettes*.

Le Drugstore crowd spawned the era of *minets* or 'trendies'. The term first appeared around 1965 to describe the mass of French teenagers who were obsessed with British clothes and music, and the American music that had influenced the Brits. The *minets* regarded themselves as a cut above the *yé-yés*, the ordinary French adolescent pop fans who preferred a more commercial soundtrack.

Style provider for the *minets* was Renoma, a tailor and garment-making business run by Simon Cressy on Rue Notre-Dame-de-Nazareth near Place de la Republique. His sons Maurice and Michel Cressy encouraged him to make trousers like the *marinettes*, real bell-bottoms, twelve inches wide at the bottom. These were the prototypes of 1970s flares.

Using a suit pattern from England, Renoma then produced sharp-looking three-button fitted suits, with a slightly concave 'pagoda' shape to the narrow shoulders and deep twelve-inch vents. 'My father called them "chimney sweep" suits. They literally hugged body and shoulders. There was no

Left: By spring 1966 Pierre Cardin was offering men a huge choice of suit styles, each personalised with a neat touch, such as the asymmetrical pocket flaps seen at the extreme left. It is interesting to compare this line-up with the one from London in 1931 on pages 52–3.

extra play. It was amazing,' Michel Cressy told Chenoune in an interview in the early 1990s.[7]

In flannel for winter and a lighter gabardine for summer, the Renoma suit became the uniform of the affluent *minets*. The trendiest among them were given free suits as an incentive to bring in more new clients.

There were plenty of new clients after October 1963 when Simon Cressy and his sons opened White House Renoma on Rue de la Pompe in the sixteenth arrondisement near a posh secondary school. Other boutiques followed them, and the street became the mecca for *minet* fashion between 1964 and 1968.

The classic *minet* style included fitted Renoma jackets in corduroy or velour (which had been an unconventional men's fabric until then). The colour palette was bold, too, embracing violet, green, light brown, dark brown, blue and red. Complementary Shetland wool pullovers came in explosive acid colours such as duck yellow, candy pink, pale blue and mauve. Like the British Mods who were their stylistic cousins, the *minets* presented an androgynous air and the style was carried off best on skinny teenagers.

The *minet* style, which peaked around 1966 to 1967, made a big impression on Philip Start, a lad-about-London who was to found the influential Woodhouse menswear chain in the late 1970s. 'People don't know what I'm talking about these days when I mention the French Mod look, but I used to go to clubs in London that were aimed at French *au pairs* and you'd see guys from Paris there,' he recalled in an interview with me in mid-2008. 'French performers like Sacha Distel and Alain Delon looked really good.'

The tailor of choice for many French showbiz types such as Charles Aznavour, Jean-Paul Belmondo and Roman Polanski

was Ted Lapidus. Born in 1929, he started his own business in 1950 and ten years later opened an innovative and expensive boutique called Tedd at 6 Place Victor-Hugo in the sixteenth arrondisement. By the 1970s, it had grown into a chain of thirty shops. Another French name whose influence is often overlooked, Lapidus, who had studied technical engineering in Japan, saw himself as a suit engineer and followed the school of long, slim lines, minimum padding on the jacket and flared trousers. His later offerings included safari suits and close-fitting double-breasted suits with high-fastening buttons.

A more famous devotee of the safari suit was Yves St Laurent, who introduced menswear in 1969, claiming he could not find what he wanted to wear. In 1971 he struck a deal with the large French manufacturer Bidermann to make and distribute menswear under the Saint Laurent Rive Gauche brand. YSL is possibly better remembered today for putting women in suits – or tuxedo suits at least – but his menswear has often been directional but wearable.

That description could also apply to Nino Cerruti, an Italian by birth who relocated to Paris in 1967 to start a menswear business. His family textiles business in Biella in northern Italy had been founded in 1881 and the Cerruti 1881 label became known for understated, streamlined, luxurious clothes for men. The fabrics, naturally, were always superb, something that was not lost on one of Cerruti's assistants, a young Italian called Giorgio Armani.

The French love of unisex dressing had a number of leading lights, such as Jean Cacherel, who worked with prints for shirts and blouses, and Jacques Esterel, who often worked (as did Cardin and Féruch) in knitted jersey to move away from the traditional boundaries set by woven suitings. Esterel is best remembered for two things: designing Brigitte Bardot's pink gingham wedding dress for her 1959 marriage to actor Jacques Charrier and proposing, in 1966, that men might want to wear skirts.

This unconventional approach to unisex fashion was revived in 1985 by Jean Paul Gaultier, who had worked for Esterel in 1971. Born in 1952, Gaultier also worked twice for Pierre Cardin, who instilled in him the idea that nothing was impossible. After starting his own womenswear business in 1976, he launched himself into menswear in 1984 and brought an attitude that was amusing and provocative at the same time. A huge fan of British street style, Gaultier would regularly be seen in a kilt and a pair of Dr Martens boots. Colin McDowell praised him highly in 1997. While admitting that 'ninety per cent of his ideas die on the catwalk', McDowell asserted that JPG was 'the only truly modern menswear designer and a world leader ... the most radical and uncompromising designer working in male fashion today. In as little as fifty years he may well be seen as the only designer of vision at the end of the twentieth century.'[8]

Gaultier's 'skirt for men' was, in fact, not a skirt, but a pair of trousers, one leg of which overlapped the other. The publicity it received was not reflected in retail sales. One undisputed commercial success from the mid-1980s was his double-breasted suit, which had exaggeratedly wide shoulders and an exaggeratedly tight fit around the hips. This almost cartoon-like silhouette, worn with wide or narrow trousers, was an international success. At Woodhouse in London, Philip Start had copies made for his own label, asking his manufacturer in Italy to put the shoulders of a 42-inch model with the lower jacket of a 38-inch model to acheive the desired distortion of proportion.

Paris was the undisputed centre of luxury menswear in the '80s. Alongside classic names such as Lanvin (which had been making menswear since the 1920s), a men's line was offered by a long roster of originally womenswear designers such as Pierre Balmain, Christian Dior, Louis Féraud, Guy Laroche, Daniel Hechter, Emanuel Ungaro, Claude Montana, Thierry Mugler and Karl Lagerfeld. For two decades Paris had also been the European base for Japanese designers such as Kenzo Takada (who arrived in 1964), Issey Miyake (whose first Paris catwalk show was in 1973), Yohji Yamamoto and Rei Kawakubo, creator of Comme des Garçons, who brought an intellectual and monochrome approach to suit design.

Making Paris a twice-yearly destination of the world's menswear buyers was Sehm (Salon International de l'Habillement Masculin), a trade show that had started out with eighty exhibitors in 1960 as an annual event, but started running two sessions a year (January and September) from 1971. By the late 1990s, it had 700 exhibitors from all sectors of the trade and ran alongside the twice-yearly Paris catwalk shows, which, as well as French names, attracted international designers such as Ralph Lauren and Paul Smith.

In the 1990s the menswear fashion pendulum swung towards Milan as brands such as Armani, Versace and Gucci looked more sexy and/or commercial than those offered by Paris. Due to the decline in the French independent boutique sector, Sehm itself closed, leaving Pitti Uomo in Florence as the marketplace for better-end menswear.

Paris is still the powerhouse of the luxury end of the market, as it is the base of two major luxury conglomerates: Louis Vuitton-Moët Hennessy (LVMH), whose interests include Christian Dior, Louis Vuitton, Kenzo and Givenchy; and PPR (formerly Pinault-Printemps-Redoute), whose interests include Gucci, Yves Saint Laurent and Alexander McQueen. It remains a small world that is still able to spring surprises. In 2000, Hedi Slimane, former menswear designer at YSL, moved across to Dior Homme and with his early collections showed a super-slim, very closely cut silhouette that, so far, has been the most influential suit look of the new century.

"... so I've took out my big white handkerchief and folded it carefully over my left lapel. I was wearing a navy-blue lightweight suit, in a material called Tonik, made by Dormeuil, and I didn't want it spoiling. I don't care whether a bird wears Max Factor Mattfilm or Outdoor Girl from Woolworth's, if she starts purring it up against your lapel, it won't look the better for it."

Alfie Elkins, in *Alfie* by Bill Naughton

Right: Launched by the Anglo-French firm Dormeuil in 1957, Tonik, an expensive blend of 41% wool and 59% mohair, was the ultimate 'two-tone' fabric for the most luxurious Mod suits. Today the adjective 'tonic' is often applied erroneously to any fabric with a hint of iridescence or sheen.

Tonik*
BY DORMEUIL

*Ideal for
Social
Climbers*

Left: Yves St Laurent in his studio in September 1966 before he unleashed the safari suit on menswear.

Above right: Jean Paul Gaultier has been distorting the proportions of men's suits to almost cartoon proportions since the 1980s. Here, in 1984, he models his own roomy creation.

Below right: The super-slimline silhouette designed by Hedi Slimane for Dior Homme was one of the strongest fashion trends in the early years of the twenty-first century and brought many young men back into suits. This version is from Autumn/Winter 2002.

Above: Ted Lapidus, seen here in the late 1960s, studied as a technical engineer in Japan and brought a rigorous discipline to his designing of suits. His look was typically long, with slim jackets contrasted with flared trousers.

Right: French expertise in weaving fancy fabrics found bold expression in the fashion suits of the 1970s, as seen here in an autumn 1970 suit from Chauvet.

The Dormeuil suits

The Anglo-French company Dormeuil has been producing and distributing fine fabrics since 1842 and the backbone of its business has always been men's suitings. In addition to its high-quality production, the firm is remarkable for its long-standing commitment to promoting its fine wares and fine tailoring through memorable advertisements. As well as promoting its own fabric qualities such as Sportex and Tonik, Dormeuil's extensive marketing efforts reminded men of the power of dressing well. Today the Dormeuil name is found on a collection of ready-made suits as well as on its traditional suitings.

Above: Dormeuil's London-based marketing chief Peter T Watson was responsible for the amusing and striking images in which the man (modelled on James Bond) always got the attention of the girl. This mid-1960s ad is for Tonik.

Left: Undiluted, timeless Gallic insouciance from Dormeuil in a typically stylish illustration from the celebrated artist René Gruau.

Above: Another superb period piece from the mid-1960s, again promoting Tonik.

Left: The Sportex fabric, introduced in 1922, is a plain weave of pure twisted wool. Available in more than 400 designs, it became known as 'the cloth of champions, the champion of cloths'.

chapter SEVEN Lost in Music

There's no show-off like a showbiz show-off. Since at least the Middle Ages, performers have used their position as an excuse to dress up, to present a theatrical sense of dressing. Even off the stage, entertainers felt the need or the responsibility to put on a show.

Over the past hundred years, the suit has served the music business well, either as a stylish uniform for large bands and small groups or as an individual statement for a star performer. There can have been few other men who bought as many suits as some top stars. Singers and musicians have set trends, revived trends and become icons on the strength of their tailoring. And it's amazing how many once-scruffy rockers graduate to a sharp suit once they've hit the big time.

Music-hall and vaudeville performers set the trend at the beginning of the twentieth century; audiences wanted their idols to be well turned out. In immaculate matching outfits, the early ragtime bands and dance bands of the pre-First World War era set high standards that continued for decades. Louis Armstrong, born on 4 August 1901, was a stylish dresser on and off the stage for fifty years and his various bands were consistently dapper. Edward Kennedy Ellington was born on 29 April 1899 into a well-to-do middle-class black family in Washington DC. By the age of fourteen he was using his own money from a summer job to buy his clothes and he was nicknamed 'Duke' Ellington by the time he was in his mid-teens on account of his narcissistic devotion to his appearance. His parents

encouraged him to be an achiever and taught him pride in his race and a duty to serve it well. '[Duke] was as sharp as a Gillette blade. His mother and father drummed that in to him. His father was a fine-looking man, polished,' recalled jazz drummer Sonny Greer.[1] Duke's father, James Edward Ellington, was variously a butler, a caterer and a blueprinter in the shipyards, yet still chose to wear spats and gloves.

Bill Basie, born on 21 August 1904, was another jazz legend whose wardrobe and demeanour earned him an aristocratic sobriquet. From the early 1920s onwards Count Basie's dressing was as precise and correct as his piano playing. Popular music proved to be a bridge between cultures and classes in the early decades of the twentieth century. During the Prohibition era of the 1920s – the Jazz Age – wealthy whites went up to the clubs of Harlem and black American musicians made the transatlantic trip to Europe. Armstrong toured Europe in 1932 and 1934. Duke Ellington made his first visit to Europe in 1933. Such exchanges opened up different strata of societies to each other's influences; even the hottest jazz musician of the era wanted to adopt the suit, the uniform of the gentleman.

Some performers – such as Scots-born vocalist and dancer Jack Buchanan, 'the British Fred Astaire' – crisscrossed the Atlantic regularly and became celebrated for their wardrobe as much as for their act. Born in Helensburgh on the River Clyde on 2 April 1891, Buchanan made his Broadway debut in 1924; his whole persona, on and off the stage, was that of a debonair man-about-town. Reflecting the formal dress their well-to-do audiences often still wore for theatre-going, the performers were regularly seen in black-tie suits.

Like their Hollywood movie counterparts, the music stars of the pre-Second World War period felt they owed it to their audiences to be seen as dapper fashion plates at all times, on stage and off. Their desire for the spotlight – literal and

"... His clothes are loud, but never square.
It will make or break him so he's
got to buy the best, cause he's
a dedicated follower of fashion."

'Dedicated Follower of Fashion', The Kinks

figurative – encouraged them to wear the latest styles, displaying far more of the peacock tendency than a regular guy in the street ever would or could. The first of the modern species of popular music star, Francis Albert Sinatra, was an enthusiastic clothes-horse from his earliest days; American-Italians needed no encouragement to dress up.

From the late 1950s, as rock'n'roll and pop music of all shades became a huge industry, it became a route to fast wealth for poor but talented kids. It is interesting to note how many working-class performers, ranging from doo-wop vocal groups to electric blues guitarists, chose the suit as the outward sign that they had arrived. The quintessential 1950s success story, Elvis Aaron Presley, spent significant amounts of his income from his early blue-collar jobs at Lansky Brothers clothiers in Memphis, where he bought clothes he hoped would make him stand out as a singer. In a story reported by rock writer Paul Gorman, before the big time happened, Elvis told co-owner Bernard Lansky, 'I don't have no money now, but whenever I get rich I'm going to buy you out.' Lansky replied, 'Don't buy me out, just buy from me.'[2]

Significantly, the clientele for Lansky Brothers on Beale Street was almost exclusively black, so it wasn't just the black music that Elvis was borrowing. The King remained an innovative clothes-horse until the end. His gold suit on the sleeve of the 1959 album *50,000,000 Elvis Fans Can't Be Wrong* is surely the boldest statement ever saying, 'I've made it!' The clothes in his thirty-one movies were almost always better than the acting or the script. With a brocade evening suit, whose tone-on-tone pattern came to life under the photographers' flash bulbs, he had one of the best groom's outfits ever for his Las Vegas wedding to Priscilla on 1 May 1967. And his 1968 NBC comeback special yielded some fantastic looks, from the sexy black leather two-piece to the Southern gentlemen's white frock-coat suit that he wore for the show's finale.

For all its revolutionary fervour, and its presumed threats to world order, the rock'n'roll boom was very well dressed. It is difficult to find an on-stage photograph of the likes of Little Richard, Fats Domino, Chuck Berry, Bo Diddley or Buddy Holly and The Crickets when they are not wearing a suit, or at least a tuxedo and black trousers. But we shouldn't be surprised – these were all poor working-class boys and dressing up was a statement that they were moving up. At least Little Richard Penniman was showman enough to sport an updated zoot suit as he pounded the 88s.

The top R & B and blues performers, such as B B King, Bobby 'Blue' Bland, Muddy Waters and John Lee Hooker, went for a smart, sharp look, too. Thousands of rural blacks like them who had moved up north before, during and after the Second World War swapped their farmers' overalls for plain dark suits when they reached Chicago, Cincinnati, Detroit and the rest of the northern urban centres. Simple suits like this were the cheapest to buy, but they indicated a new social ascension of the black working class. Twenty-five years later, Jake and Elwood, the Blues Brothers, would copy the lean and hip look of John Lee Hooker for their own trademark suits.

In the metropolitan cities up north, the craze for close-harmony groups in the doo-wop or pop styles was championed by Americans of Italian descent such as Dion

Above: One of the men who were in at The Birth of The Cool, Miles Davis, seen here in 1961 or 1962, was a kingpin of Modern Jazz. The Modernists had their style and their name adapted and adopted by the Mods.

By the time The Beatles reached the US in February 1964, they had dropped their Cardin-inspired collarless jackets for more conventional black suits. The one-time leather-jacketed rockers were beginning to look a little bit Mod. American players of Modern Jazz such as Miles Davis had given the movement its name and its stylistic direction. Born into a prosperous family in 1926, Davis had the lithe, lean build of a cat and he looked ultra-sharp in his Italian-inspired, body-conscious suits.

The spare yet sharp profile of the Mod suit owed a lot to the Continental style that had been a strong fashion story in the late 1950s and early 1960s. It was polished to new heights of cool by the clan of good-looking and gorgeous-sounding male groups that were gathered at 2648 West Grand Boulevard in Detroit by one Berry Gordy. It was part of the corporate philosophy at his Tamla-Motown company that his stars – both male and female – should attend dancing and deportment lessons. The Four Tops, The Temptations, Smokey Robinson and The Miracles, The Isley Brothers, Marvin Gaye, Stevie Wonder and The Contours, not to mention the Funk Brothers house band, always but always looked immaculate. They caused a sensation when, under the encouragement of Dusty Springfield, they visited the UK in 1965 and thrilled viewers of the top TV pop show *Ready Steady Go!*

and the Belmonts and Frankie Valli and The Four Seasons, plus numerous black groups such as The Platters, The Flamingos, The Coasters and Frankie Lymon and The Teenagers – once again the tailors were kept busy. A sharp, often shiny suit was the essential uniform, with body contours that were as close as the harmonies.

Over in jolly old England, early rockers such as Cliff Richard, Billy Fury and Adam Faith took their stylistic lead from their American heroes. Cliff's backing group The Shadows dressed in matching slim-Jim suits as they performed their neat footwork routines. Close variations of this look can be found on hundreds of publicity shots and album covers of the first decade of modern pop and rock – just check out Freddie and The Dreamers, The Merseybeats, The Easybeats, Herman's Hermits, The Searchers, The Swinging Blue Jeans ...

Just as Teddy Boys in the 1950s had adopted the rock'n'roll genre, so Mods in the 1960s embraced Tamla, soul, R & B, and danced to it, as The Who recalled on their *Quadrophenia* album, in 'zoot suit, white jacket with side vents five inches long'. While the terminology is incorrect – these most definitely were not zoot suits – the precision of the vents' length is typical of the exacting standards Mods set themselves. This was one of the most narcissistic cults ever, even though most of its adherents were working-class youths.

Right: Somehow this silk or mohair extravaganza would not look right on a man called Ronald Wycherley, but once he had changed his name to Billy Fury, everything was perfect. Here he rocks Wembley in 1962.

Like the Teddy Boy look, the Mod style has had an impressive longevity, not least in that most elitist of sub-genres, the Northern Soul scene. Devoted to fast-tempo tracks from obscure American soul performers, the early Northern Soul fan in the late 1960s and early 1970s had a rigorous dress code. As John Bollen, a regular at The Twisted Wheel club in Manchester and the Blackpool Mecca, revealed: 'If you wore a suit, it had to be three-button. It had to be buttoned at the top button. If it was buttoned on the middle button, you were a div. You had to have a single vent at the back that went to the waist. You had to have flaps on the pockets that were slightly sloping. You had to have a ticket pocket on the right-hand side. It was all in the details.'[3]

As the pop boom of the 1960s evolved into the rock boom of the 1970s, so the role of the suit moved with it. Rock aristocracy began to dress like, well, real aristocracy, in lavish and outlandish suits, as fashion replaced classic looks. The 'Dedicated Follower of Fashion' lampooned by The Kinks in 1966 – which was rich coming from them, as they were no strangers to frills and extravagant fabrics themselves – became the Decadent Follower of Fashion in the early 1970s. The Rolling Stones were the leaders of the louche look, with Mick and the boys adopting an early version of the Eurotrash aesthetic. In keeping with their early policy of not wearing a band uniform, the group all wore different takes of the same vibe, but could be relied upon to don a suit for a court appearance or to get married. Over the years, when he emerged from behind the drum kit, former Mod Charlie Watts turned out to be by far the best-dressed Stone.

A fine example of using the suit to distort one's image was offered by Bob Dylan on his first electric tour of Europe in 1966. Leaving his previous protest-singer's garb at home, he prowled the stage in front of The Band in a curious loudly checked suit with memorably narrow trousers.

Another show-stopping suit was the blue DB sported by Otis Redding as he and Booker T and The MGs – always a suited-and-booted combo at that time – set the stage alight at the Monterey Pop Festival on 17 June 1967 in front of an audience of prototype Californian hippies. The juxtaposition neatly summed up the direction of the musical wardrobe for a good part of the 1970s – the rock crowd dressing down in denim and hand-me-downs, while the soul boys remained true to dressing to impress in a kaleidoscope of suits. Extravagant colours, alarming synthetic fabrics and proportions that fitted and flared as never before were the order of the day for most of the decade.

The glam-rock years of the mid-1970s saw suits appearing as previously unheard of statements of extravagance. New tailors such as Tommy Nutter of Savile Row – who was part-financed in his early days by singer Cilla Black – won the patronage of a whole clutch of rock and pop royalty, most prominently Elton John. Another diffraction from the prism of glam rock was the 'art school' influence of Roxy Music. Led by ex-soul boy Bryan Ferry, Roxy could do glam but was even more important in launching the craze for nostalgic recreations of fashions from the 1930s and 1940s; the track '2HB' from Roxy's eponymous first album in 1972 was nothing to do with pencils and everything to do with Ferry saluting one of his heroes, Humphrey Bogart.

With London-based designer Antony Price as his tailor, Ferry was rarely seen in the same thing twice and engendered a

Right: On his 1966 tour of Europe, Bob Dylan outraged his folk fans by giving half his concerts over to blistering rock, backed by The Hawks, later known as The Band. His curious super-slim houndstooth suit – which looks like it's made from a women's coat fabric – signalled a new direction for Bob as surely as his amplified Fender guitar.

fanatical following of well-dressed fans that plundered the charity shops for old double-breasted suits. I know; I was one of them.

Other nostalgic musical adventurers of the early 1970s included The Pasadena Roof Orchestra from the UK and the New York-based vocal quartet Manhattan Transfer, which both reflected the decade's interest in looking back to a more elegant age.

A key influencer who continues to champion suits to this day is David Bowie. Having achieved massive success as the space cadet Ziggy Stardust, Bowie surprised his audience by appearing on the cover of his 1974 album *David Live* in a memorable suit with an exaggeratedly short, boxy DB jacket and wide trousers. He'd worn the suit on the American tour during which the album was recorded. (See also pages 160–3).

Bowie's 1975 album *Young Americans* saw him adopt a modern soul-boy persona, from which it was a small shuffle on the dance floor to the immaculate image of Chic, the New York group that defined a new sound and a new look in the late 1970s. A suit, shirt and tie was a wholly appropriate outfit for the core audience of Black Urban Professionals – the Buppies.

In the 1980s in their wake came smooth soul singers such as Luther Vandross and Alexander O'Neill, whose large bodies were ideally shaped to carry off the 'athletic' cut of the decade's wide-shouldered DB suits.

Left: August Darnell's alter-ego was Kid Creole, who, backed by The Coconuts, spearheaded a revival of the zoot-suit look in the early 1980s. This was only the most extreme example of an interest in vintage styles during this period.

On the face of it, the 1976 outburst of punk in the UK had little to do with wearing suits, but its development into 'alternative' rock produced a number of bands that picked up on a 1960s Mod or ska vibe, notably The Jam and the Two-Tone posse of The Selecter, The Beat and The Specials. Inner-city young men were once again expressing their identity in a neat three-button SB suit. The 1979 film based on The Who's concept album *Quadrophenia* was a massive boost for the neo-Mod look.

Another, more narrow, wave of nostalgia in the early 1980s saw the zoot suit revived by August Darnell, a.k.a. Kid Creole, leader of funk group The Coconuts. His revival of the long jacket and baggy trousers of the 1930s and 1940s found a few high-profile adherents in the trendy clubs of London, but this remained a minority sport.

More conventional suits could still pack a visual punch. The German electronic quartet Kraftwerk looked totally different from their New Romantic contemporaries in their pointedly anonymous business suits in the late 1970s. Many of the New Romantic bands graduated to suits when they tired of the billowy fake-Regency look; Antony Price was again the tailor of choice for bands such as Ultravox, Duran Duran and Simple Minds.

The growth of the designer labels – mainly Italian – in the 1980s attracted certain members of the rock aristocracy, with Gianni Versace in particular winning over suit fans Elton John and Phil Collins. Later, legendary clothes-horse Eric Clapton would favour Armani.

Since the early 1990s the emergence of a crop of younger, London-based bespoke tailors – Richard James, Timothy Everest, William Hunt, Mark Powell, Nick Tentis – has coincided with a greater readiness for working-class lads to dress up for special occasions such as weddings. This trend

was itself influenced by the smart ensembles worn by boy bands such as Take That and Boyzone, which were typically dark frock-coat-length jackets and neat trousers, worn with a shirt and tie of similarly dark hues. George Michael was one of the longer-established names who graduated to wearing a suit as his preferred stage garb. Into the new millennium, American hip-hop stars such as Andre and Sean 'P Diddy' Combs began to prefer the more restrained elegance of a well-cut suit to oversized sportswear and vulgar bling.

The generally dressed-down 1990s were superseded in the early years of the millennium when the super-slim line of Hedi Slimane's Dior Homme collection was picked up by bands such as Franz Ferdinand and The Rakes. Slimane's styles are also worn by David Bowie, who was himself a huge influence on the young Frenchman. Remembering the effect the *David Live* album cover had on him, Slimane told

Paul Gorman: 'I must have stared at the cover of him in that light-blue suit with braces at least five million times. The sense of transformation you get with Bowie is amazing.'[4]

That's the power of the suit in rock.

Above: From 1962, Tamla-Motown's power trio The Isley Brothers show that the label's style and deportment lessons represented money well spent.

Right: The Hardest Working Man In Show Business, James Brown, had a lifelong preoccupation with being immaculately dressed. Despite the incredible energy of his shows, he often wore three-piece suits, as seen here in 1964.

Overleaf: Waiting to perform on The Ed Sullivan Show on 9 February, 1964 – their US TV debut – Paul and John (and Ringo at the back) go for that classic standby – the neat black suit, white shirt and narrow tie.

Left: In 1965 Rod Stewart and Long John Baldry were together in a band called Steampacket. It was a Mod band, in case you hadn't guessed.

Above: Re-made. Re-modelled: Antony Price exaggerated the proportions of classic men's tailoring to help create an unforgettable persona for Bryan Ferry in the early days of Roxy Music in the 1970s.

" *I dig rock 'n' roll music.*
I can do The Twine and The Jerk.
I wear strictly Continental suits
And high-collared shirts.
I've got a reputation of being
Gentle but bold.
And that's why they call me
Agent Double-O Soul, baby,
Agent Double-O Soul."

Edwin Starr, 'Agent 00 Soul', 1965

Left: *Kraftwerk* means 'power plant' in German. In the 1970s the four electronic music pioneers brought a powerful new sound to pop and a new interpretation to pop 'power dressing'.

Above: Alex Kapranos of Franz Ferdinand maintains rock's links with fine tailoring with his slimline suits. He was an early adopter of Hedi Slimane's pared-down look for Dior Homme.

Left: Paul Weller and Bruce Foxton of The Jam, here photographed in 1978, brought a Mod sensibility to the post-punk alternative scene with their slim, monochrome suits.

Right: Duran Duran turned to the old master, Antony Price, when they wanted sharp suits. Simon Le Bon and John Taylor wear them well in 1983.

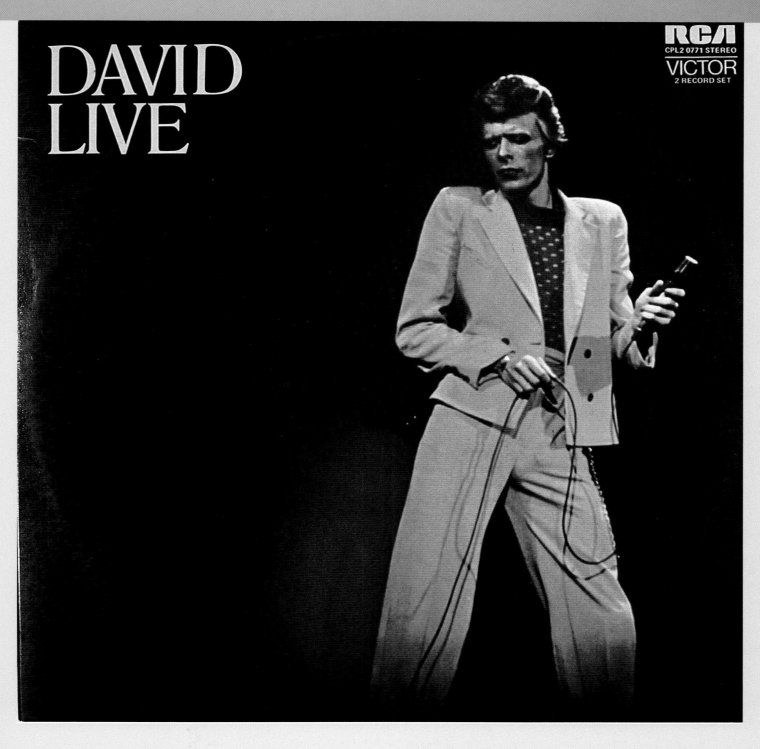

DAVID
LIVE

RCA
CPL2 0771 STEREO
VICTOR
2 RECORD SET

David Bowie is a hero of the suit. He appeared on an early album cover in a woman's dress. He dressed as space cadet Ziggy Stardust for a significant part of his career. But the chameleon Bowie has shown a remarkable loyalty to suits throughout his long years at the top of the rock hierarchy. Here we celebrate a few pin-ups from his tailoring wardrobe.

Above: Having said farewell to Ziggy Stardust and Aladdin Sane, Bowie entered his Plastic Soul phase in 1974 with this striking image on the cover of *David Live*. The short box jacket and baggy trousers distort the usual balance of the suit.

Left: This three-piece tailcoat suit dates from 2002. These days, Bowie is rarely seen out of a suit, on or off stage.

Above: The exaggeratedly sculptural effect of this suit from around 1973 may have been created by fashion designer Freddie Burretti. Bowie would often reprise the tight jacket and baggy trouser look.

Above right: Another idiosyncratic interpretation of the suit proportions from 1973, possibly by Antony Price or Freddie Burretti.

Opposite: As keen as mustard: a typically imaginative tailoring exercise for Bowie from around 1974. If the wide shawl collar wasn't enough, check out the curious 'teardrop' bell sleeves.

chapter
EIGHT
The Magic of the Movies

The big screen has presented a wardrobe of delights for suit lovers since the early part of the twentieth century. Once Auguste and Louis Lumière showed their cinématographe system to the public in Lyons in 1895, it was only a few years before the potential of the new medium began to be realised. By the end of the first decade of the 1900s, the pioneers of the movie industry were settling in southern California. The power of the suit as a 'statement' outfit was soon to be made. In 1914, the first character to be instantly recognisable by his suit – Charlie Chaplin's 'Tramp' – made his scruffy debut in a short called *Kid Auto Races*. His old-fashioned black morning suit characterised him as a loner, one who did not quite belong.

Normally the audience expected the hero to be well dressed, but from the beginning of the 1930s, just as the Great Depression began, Hollywood showed that crime paid, at least for a while. Starting a trend that continues to the present day, cinema suggested that the baddie had the best suits, rather like the Devil having the best tunes. In 1930 at least two dozen gangster films were produced by Hollywood, most memorably *Little Caesar*, in which an immaculately turned-out Edward G Robinson as Rico Bandello ruled over a criminal empire. The following year James Cagney was Tom Powers, *The Public Enemy*. He was the sort of Chicago hoodlum that mashed a grapefruit into the face of a woman over the breakfast table, proving that being well dressed did not make him a gentleman. In 1932 Paul Muni as Tony Camonte in the title role of *Scarface* took his lapels to new widths, emphasising the notion that the bad guy tended towards flashy show rather than subtle elegance. As Scarface's right-hand man, George Raft fitted the bill as a nasty heavy as well as his suits fitted him.

The well-dressed villain became a staple of the thriller genre. In Alfred Hitchcock's *Rebecca* in 1940, George Sanders appeared as the Savile Row-suited blackmailer Jack Favell. You can tell he's a bad 'un from the moment he appears in his immaculate chalk-striped DB suit; he looks the sort of man who would wear brown suede shoes with it.

The suave cad was a persona Sanders would reprise in the 1950 Oscar winner *All About Eve*, in which he played Addison de Witt, a bitchy theatre critic who effectively narrates the picture. Two of Hollywood's most celebrated costume designers, Edith Head and Charles LeMaire, shared the Costume Design Oscar for this movie.

Back again in 1940, suit fans had a treat when James Stewart jousted with Cary Grant for the attentions of Katharine Hepburn in *The Philadelphia Story*, a clever comedy of manners involving the well-to-do set that most of the cinema-going public had no chance of joining. Grant's rather stuffy character is contrasted nicely against the more easy-going Stewart, who wore his SB suits very well indeed.

While Stewart is remembered as much for his Western roles these days, Cary Grant remains many people's idea of the immaculate Hollywood star. Making his films in the days when male stars were expected to supply their own clothes, he never disappointed his audience. Although he is usually the hero, in Hitchcock's 1941 thriller *Suspicion* Grant plays Johnnie Aysgarth, a debonair English con man who marries the shy but wealthy Lina McLaidlaw (Joan Fontaine). The plot centres around whether Aysgarth will kill his wife; the scene in which a DB-suited Grant takes a suspicious glass of milk upstairs to his wife is chilling. Surely someone so well turned out can't be a poisoner …

Despite his reputation as a tailoring pin-up, Grant maintained he had little interest in clothes. His father, who, coincidentally, had been a presser in a Bristol clothing factory, drummed into his son that he should always buy the best clothes he could, but should choose classic styles that

wouldn't date. Grant has become associated with the suit for very good reasons – in the comedy thriller *Charade* (1963) he even takes a shower in his trademark dark SB while trying to get some peace away from Regina Lambert, played by Audrey Hepburn. 'Wearing this suit during washing helps protect its shape,' he jokes to a bemused Regina.

In 1959, again with Hitchcock in the director's chair, Grant was even more out of place in a suit. As ad executive Roger Thornhill in the stylish if slightly implausible thriller *North by Northwest,* Grant is chased across fields in the middle of the countryside by a crop-spraying plane. He is an urban man, both out of place and in danger in a distinctly rural setting, a point emphasised by Grant's elegant – and in the circumstances somewhat impractical – grey suit.

Other movies have employed the same notion – or a reversal of it – to strong effect. In John Sturges' 1955 masterpiece *Bad Day at Black Rock,* a one-armed stranger called James J Macreedy, played by Spencer Tracy, comes to a small town in Arizona and uncovers a murderous skeleton in the community closet. Tracy, in his dark city suit and with one arm, looks startlingly out of place, especially when contrasted with the latter-day cowboys pitted against him, led by Lee Marvin at his malevolent best.

Twelve years later the stranger in the black suit became the black stranger in the black suit when Sidney Poitiers' city detective Virgil Tibbs became embroiled in a murder investigation in a steamy Mississippi town. In the Norman Jewison film *In the Heat of the Night* Poitier was black when those in power around him were white. He was apparently cool while others sweltered. And in his neat two-piece he was slickly dressed in contrast to his adversaries, most noticeably Rod Steiger's bulky police chief Bill Gillespie. This gripping drama won the Best Picture Oscar and the Best Actor award for Steiger.

Previous page: The first two *Godfather* movies from 1972 and 1974 together represent the best-dressed film adventure, covering menswear across most decades of the twentieth century. Here Al Pacino is a brooding Michael Corleone.

Above: Quentin Tarantino's *Reservoir Dogs* (1992) provided one of the best men's suit group shots since *Ocean's Eleven* in 1960 and heralded a pronounced shift towards simple, even austere, tailored outfits.

In 1969, in *Coogan's Bluff,* Clint Eastwood reversed the scenario as a dour Arizona deputy looking very out of place in his updated cowboy suit around the mean streets and nightclubs of New York, trying to find a fugitive. Eastwood's lawman loner, always ready to bend the rules, was the prototype for his later incarnation of Dirty Harry Callahan, who preferred a very anonymous wardrobe. All the jacket had to do was accommodate a Magnum 44.

Vying for top billing as best-dressed film of the late 1960s was Norman Jewison's stylish 1968 caper *The Thomas Crown Affair.* In the title role, Steve McQueen played a very successful but bored financier who organised the robbery of his own bank. The then largely unknown Faye Dunaway was cast opposite him as Vicki Anderson, an insurance investigator who is soon on to Crown. Crown is a banker with attitude and wears the most brilliant suits, almost always three-piece outfits, as he plays cat-and-mouse with his equally well-dressed pursuer. Reportedly McQueen wore the suits a lot before filming began to get used to the feel of fine tailoring – he was more of a slacks and polo-shirt man in real life. Ron Postal received the plaudits as the provider of McQueen's wardrobe, but Douglas Hayward, the London showbiz tailor, actually designed and made them.

A year earlier Dunaway had been the gorgeous female lead in Arthur Penn's *Bonnie and Clyde,* a groundbreaking film that revived interest in 1930s fashions while taking the

portrayal of on-screen violence to a new level of realism. As Depression-era bank robbers Bonnie Parker and Clyde Barrow, Dunaway and her co-star Warren Beatty looked stylishly splendid, thanks to the costumes designed by Theadora van Runkle on what was her first movie. The film was nominated for the Costume Design Oscar, but it went that year to *Camelot* – the DB suits were outgunned by Dark Ages armour.

Although the Oscar system dated back to 1927 (the first Awards ceremony, covering films from 1927 and 1928, was held in May 1929) the Academy of Motion Picture Arts and Sciences did not add a category for Costume Design until 1948, when there were separate deliberations for black-and-white films and for colour films. The two categories existed for most years until 1967. The first winners in 1948 were, respectively, *Hamlet* and *Joan of Arc* – it was another good year for medieval armour.

Another early nominee for the Costume Design statuette was Irene Sharaff, for the 1955 musical *Guys and Dolls*, one of the best films for ensemble playing in suits. In the 158-minute romp the lowlife characters from Damon Runyan's stories of New York street life were brought to the screen in striking colour and sound by a team of gamblers led by Sky Masterson (played by Marlon Brando) and 'good old reliable' Nathan Detroit (Frank Sinatra). Sinatra's fancy stripe one-button SB with wide shoulders and peaked lapels is a memorable suit. One can rely on characters with names such as Big Jule (pronounced Julee), Harry the Horse, Society Max, Angie the Ox and Liverlips Louie to be no strangers to the tailor's shop.

Left: A one-button SB with peaked lapels proves lucky with the ladies for Sky Masterson (Marlon Brando) in this publicity still from *Guys and Dolls* (1955).

Above: In *Chinatown* (1974), J J Gittes (Jack Nicholson) showed what the best-dressed 1930s private eye should be wearing. Faye Dunaway looks impressed.

From the mid-1950s onwards it was hard to detect where Sinatra's off-screen persona stopped and his on-screen one began. With his Rat Pack pals – Dean Martin, Joey Bishop, Sammy Davis Jr and Peter Lawford – it seemed to be a never-ending caper of broads, booze, bands, ballads and beautiful threads. Often dressed by US showbiz tailor Sy Devore, the guys favoured shiny suits featuring mohair or sharkskin fabrics (which have nothing to do with fish leather – it's just a crisp wool or wool-blend weave). With a strong Italian influence, the sharp lines were characterised by narrow lapels and jetted pockets, and flat-fronted trousers without turn-ups. The 1960 original version of *Ocean's Eleven* saw the gang in fine form in outfits credited to costume designer Howard Shoup. The Las Vegas heist yarn was revived in 2001 with George Clooney and Brad Pitt, but their outfits were largely forgettable compared with the original. The final scene, in which the dejected gang wander down the street after their money has been cremated in error, is a fine parade of early 1960s style.

There was more than a hint of an Italian influence in *La Dolce Vita* and *8½* (for which Piero Gheradi won the black-and-white Costume Design Oscars for 1961 and 1963 respectively). Both starred Marcello Mastroianni, for many people the epitome of Italian cool. In the first he was a gossip

columnist, in the second a movie director (widely accepted to represent the two movies' director Federico Fellini).

A decade later the Italian theme continued – and how – in *The Godfather,* Francis Ford Coppola's sweeping epic looking at the organised crime empire run by the Corleone dynasty. Although the 1972 film won the Oscar for Best Picture and Marlon Brando took the Best Actor prize, this feast of sartorial excellence inexplicably was beaten to the Costume Design Oscar by *Travels With My Aunt,* a film of a Graham Greene novel.

Coupled with *The Godfather II* from 1974, this pair of gems showcases the best of Italo-American tailoring over a sixty-year period, from before the First World War to the mid-1970s. Is there a single central character that isn't always superbly clothed? My favourite suits are the slightly old-fashioned ones that Michael Corleone (Al Pacino) wears while hiding out in Sicily. But the films prove one thing – that crime buys you a great wardrobe. Anna Hill Johnstone deserves the accolades as costume designer for the series; she suggested to Coppola that costume changes should be kept to a minimum, which is why certain characters are seen in the same outfit for long periods.

The Godfather II was nominated for the Costume Design Oscar for 1974 but the Academy's members went for another iconic nostalgic piece, *The Great Gatsby,* directed by Jack Clayton. The film's costume designer Theoni V Aldredge used Ralph Lauren's actual collection of that year for the men's outfits. Robert Redford's Jay Gatsby, all the other male characters and all the extras wore Ralph Lauren. Scott Fitzgerald's 1925 novel famously describes his doomed hero as wearing 'a gorgeous pink rag of a suit'; that was the only one that had to be specially made for the film. As well as giving Ralph Lauren's relatively new menswear business a huge boost, *The Great Gatsby* was a central part of the

> *"I kept the same suit for six years and the same dialogue. They just changed the title of the picture and the leading lady."* Robert Mitchum

nostalgia for the 1920s and 1930s that hit popular culture in the early 1970s. It made a nice alternative to disco styles.

Completing an amazing trio of suit lovers' specials in 1974 was the unforgettable *Chinatown*. Director Roman Polanski and costume director Anthea Sylbert dressed J J 'Jake' Gittes (Jack Nicholson) in a series of fine suits that still made him look good after he had had his nostrils slit by a diminutive hoodlum without a sense of humour (played by Polanski himself). Whether in DB chalk-stripes with peaked lapels and a waistcoat, a white linen summer suit or a lightweight SB with notched lapels, Gittes was one well-dressed private dick. As Evelyn Mulwray, Faye Dunaway (yes, her again) was as stylish an accessory as ever.

Another nostalgic tale with great suits was *The Sting*, from 1973, in which Paul Newman and Robert Redford portray Depression-era con artists with a fine sense of style. As well as picking up the Best Picture Oscar, *The Sting* earned costume designer Edith Head one of her record-setting eight Academy Awards. It was the first mainly male film to win the costume Oscar. 'The costumes started a whole new trend in male fashion,' recalled Head. 'Suddenly men were wearing shirts with band collars, two-tone shoes and newspaper-boy caps. They brought back chalk-stripe suits. It was fascinating. I don't remember a male cast having such an impact on fashion.'[1]

Across the Atlantic, British villainy was just as well dressed. In Mike Hodges' disturbing 1971 gangster flick *Get Carter*, Jack Carter (played by Michael Caine) returns to his native Newcastle following the suspicious death of his brother. Not only has Jack lost his Geordie accent, but he's also acquired a very smart London wardrobe. The well-dressed thug was dressed by Caine's own tailor, Douglas Hayward, whose long list of celebrity clients included Roger Moore, David Niven, Peter Sellers, Terence Stamp and Patrick Lichfield.

Hayward's own playboy lifestyle is said to have inspired the character of Alfie Elkins, whom Caine played in the 1966 film *Alfie*. He actually appeared in and received prominent billing on *The Italian Job*, Caine's classic heist movie from 1969. When gang leader Charlie Croker (Caine) is released from prison, he makes an early visit to his tailor (Hayward) to be fitted with a new whistle and flute. Caine's other memorable suit-wearing leading man is Harry Palmer, the counter-espionage agent best remembered in *The Ipcress File* (1965) and *Funeral in Berlin* (1966). With his heavy-framed spectacles (heroes didn't wear glasses) and his sharp SB suits, Caine as Palmer has become a memorable 1960s image.

But the most iconic 1960s secret agent of them all is James Bond, as portrayed by Sean Connery. In six films from *Dr No* (1962) to *Diamonds are Forever* (1971), Connery set a standard that his successors George Lazenby (one film in 1969), Roger Moore (seven films, 1973–85), Timothy Dalton (two films, 1987–89), Pierce Brosnan (four films, 1995–2002) and Daniel Craig (two films so far since 2006) sometimes approached but never eclipsed.

The clean, pared-down look of the early Bond outfits is due to the original director Terence Young, who was in charge of the first two in the series, *Dr No* and *From Russia with Love*, and the fourth, *Thunderball*. A former Irish Guards officer and a dapper individual himself, he took Connery to his own tailor, Anthony Sinclair, who was based in Conduit Street, just off Savile Row. Sinclair gave Commander Bond a silhouette preferred by officers of the period – a longer jacket with a fitted waist and narrower than usual trousers. Most noticeably, he also used cloths that were much lighter than most of those used in the UK in the early 1960s. The result is that Bond, subtly, looks more modern and more international than his colleagues. The lightweight fabrics were preferred in real life by Bond's creator Ian Fleming, who was a regular visitor to the US, where lighter cloths

Above: London tailor Anthony Sinclair measures Sean Connery for one of his original James Bond suits. Sinclair was largely responsible for the memorable image of Bond in the early movies from 1962 onwards.

Left: In the latest Bond movie *Quantum of Solace* (2008), Daniel Craig projects a darker, more brutal image than any of his predecessors, but still remains well-dressed, thanks to Tom Ford's tailoring.

were adopted earlier. Normally in an SB two-piece, Bond can look almost dandyish when he goes for a waistcoat, too. He looks especially good in *Goldfinger* in a subtle Glenurquhart check, which is sufficiently well made to withstand a roll in the hay with the luscious Pussy Galore (Honor Blackman).

While George Lazenby's single performance as 007 in *On Her Majesty's Secret Service* is usually swiftly dismissed by fans, his suits were true to the Connery ethic. From 1973 and *Live and Let Die* onwards, Roger Moore drifted towards safari suits and casualwear until Douglas Hayward pulled him back to some sartorial elegance for the last films in the mid-1980s, *Octopussy* and *A View to a Kill*. Timothy Dalton never looked as comfortable in tailoring as he did in casualwear, but with *GoldenEye* (1995) the producers turned to the Italian luxury house Brioni to dress the new Bond, Pierce Brosnan. The association, which produced some elegant but largely discreet outfits, continued when Daniel Craig brought a new physicality to the role in *Casino Royale* (2006). A more body-conscious, more modern cut was provided by Tom Ford for Craig's dark SB suits in *Quantum of Solace* (2008); Bond was yet again one of the best-dressed men on the screen.

Another suit that really summed up its period was the white three-piece worn by Tony Manero (played by John Travolta) in *Saturday Night Fever* (1977). The 'pagoda' shoulders, wide lapels, nipped-in waist and tight, flared trousers have come to signify the disco era, but in fact costume designer Patrizia von Brandenstein meant for the suits to be slightly behind the prevailing fashions. Although it appeared on the film poster and is irrevocably associated with the movie, Travolta wore it for only one scene, dancing with Stephanie Mangano (Karen Lynn Gormley) to 'More Than A Woman'. Reportedly, American movie critic Gene Siskel, who had seen the movie seventeen times, sold the original white polyester suit at auction for $145,000.

Travolta apparently wanted his disco suit to be black until it was pointed out that it wouldn't be seen on the dance floor. He got his wish for a black suit (and a pink shirt) in *Grease* (1978) and then again even more notoriously in Quentin Tarantino's *Pulp Fiction* (1994) as gangster Vincent Vega, cutting a monochrome figure with fellow hitman Jules Winnfield (Samuel L Jackson). Tarantino had already established the power of the black suit, white shirt and black tie combination two years earlier in *Reservoir Dogs*, in which a jewellery raid goes horribly wrong. Such was the small budget for Tarantino's directorial debut that some of the actors supposedly wore their own clothes; Harvey Keitel reportedly wore a suit by French designer Agnès B.

The look was revived in a lighter mood in 1997 and 2002 in the two *Men in Black* movies, starring Will Smith and Tommy Lee Jones as agents fighting off aliens, or, as the posters put it, 'protecting the earth from the scum of the universe'. While not the best-fitting suits ever seen on the silver screen, their SB numbers were very in keeping with the prevailing sobriety of Prada-esque fashion styles of the time. Maybe somebody should have revived the Costume Design Oscar just for black-and-white outfits.

Right: Tony Manero (John Travolta) shows off the ideal uniform for a disco inferno in 1977. It was only worn in one scene of the movie.

Above: Thanks to Ralph Lauren's menswear collection, Robert Redford was perfectly attired for the title role of *The Great Gatsby* in 1974.

Right: He wasn't his usual Mr Nice Guy in *Notorious* (1946), but Cary Grant still kept up appearances in marvellous suits such as this one.

Left: As the amoral Alfie Elkins in *Alfie* (1966), Michael Caine usually cared more about his neat suits than the women that fell for him. The movie, along with *The Ipcress File, Get Carter* and *The Italian Job*, made Caine a 1960s style icon.

Left: Richard Gere as the male escort Julian in *American Gigolo* (1980), the movie that secured Giorgio Armani's reputation in the US and beyond.

Above: In *The Hustler* (1961), in his custom-made three-piece, Minnesota Fats (Jackie Gleason) beat Fast Eddie Felson (Paul Newman) for style as well as at pool.

Above: Warren Beatty as Clyde Barrow wearing the proceeds of one of his bank robberies. *Bonnie and Clyde* (1967) marked the start of a revival of interest in vintage styles for men.

Right: The Rat Pack in its natural habitat, on The Strip in Las Vegas, Nevada, during the filming of *Ocean's Eleven* (1960).

"You may have three-half-pence in your pocket and not a prospect in the world ... but in your new clothes you can stand on the street corner, indulging in a private daydream of yourself as Clark Gable ..."

George Orwell,

The Road to Wigan Pier

Right: Robert Redford in bold chalk stripes as the con man Johnny Hooker in *The Sting* (1973). The film was the first to win the Best Costume Oscar for primarily a menswear wardrobe. The legendary Edith Head was the costume designer.

Overleaf: Advertising executive Roger Thornhill (Cary Grant) takes evasive action from a malevolent airplane in *North by Northwest* (1959). His suit stood up remarkably well to the ordeal.

Timeline

Chas. Dalmorès

As Edward VII succeeds Queen Victoria in 1901, Europe's royalty and aristocracy begin their last decade of pre-eminent influence on men's styling. Even in his sixties, the portly monarch is a male icon in his impeccable Savile Row tailoring. The decline of the formal morning suit and the frock-coat accelerates. The rise of the bourgeoisie means that lounge suits are established as the correct uniform of the gentleman and the would-be gentleman throughout the developed world. This photograph from 1908 of French opera tenor Charles Dalmorès shows a very modern suit shape. Improved techniques in mass manufacturing, which are most advanced in the US, herald the decline of bespoke tailoring.

1910s

1920s

In Europe, more than a third of the decade is taken up with World War I, after which many European royals lose their crowns and their positions of influence. After 1918 men expect their civilian suits to be as comfortable as their military uniforms. The young and wealthy, such as these US college men in Hart Schaffner & Marx from 1917, have a varied suit wardrobe for different occasions. In warm climates such as Italy and the southern US, tailors become more adept at using lightweight cloths. The classic English look, The London Cut, developed by a Dutchman, Frederick Scholte, begins to establish the importance of the full, draped DB style, worn with wide trousers, that was to predominate for forty years.

In the postwar decade, informality in menswear increases. The Jazz Age or 'Roaring Twenties' sees a new flamboyance in menswear, almost as a reaction to the horrors of war. The early years of Hollywood make movie stars, such as Rudolph Valentino, seen here in 1925, popular style-setters. Musicians, particularly African-American ones, start to influence men's attitudes to dress. Transatlantic exchanges of styling and style icons increase. From London, Edward, Prince of Wales, later Edward VIII, conducts his one-man campaign to reduce further the rigid formality of men's tailoring. DB and SB suits still require a waistcoat. Oxford bags are a short-lived craze in the mid-1920s.

1930s 1940s

The Great Depression is a global economic disaster, but keeping up appearances in a suit remains important to many men. The Hollywood star system produces style icons such as Fred Astaire, Douglas Fairbanks Jnr and Edward G Robinson. While thousands of British men are dressed by the 'multiple tailors' such as Burton and Hepworths, leading Establishment figures like Anthony Eden and Sir Samuel Hoare, seen here in 1935, remain true to bespoke tradition. In the US, magazines such as *Apparel Arts* and *Esquire* are published for the first time, disseminating fashion information to a small but influential readership, indicating a new interest in menswear trends.

Half of the decade sees millions of men in military uniform during World War II. Civilians have to make the best of cloth rationing, which removes all extraneous details from suits. This American tweed suit from 1939 carries turn-ups, which were prohibited by wartime restrictions. Cloth is in short supply for several years after 1945. Short-lived phenomena such as the zoot suiters in the US and the *zazous* in France reveal men's desire to be noticed for their clothes. In postwar England, a few well-heeled gents attempt to revive Edwardian correctness from Savile Row. Suits are still the accepted dress for business attire and for 'Sunday best'. Bespoke tailoring continues to decline in popularity in many markets.

1950s 1960s

Rock 'n' roll heralds the arrival of teenagers as a consumer group. In the UK, the Teddy Boys are one of the first youth movements. John Stephen opens his first shop in Carnaby Street in 1957. Brioni of Italy shows that even upmarket tailors can be flamboyant, but most tailors resist change. The Italian taste for tighter and sexier suits spreads beyond the Alps. US President Truman is dapper, but many US males are anonymous in grey flannel suits. Stars such as Nat King Cole, above right, always look good, on and off the stage. Modern synthetic fibres start to infiltrate everyday menswear. Womenswear designers like Jacques Fath and Pierre Cardin begin to license their names to menswear products.

Social divisions are eroded as fashion boutiques flourish, from Blades just off Savile Row to Lord John on Carnaby Street. The new style-setters are pop stars such as The Beatles and young movie stars like Michael Caine. The Peacock Revolution, centred on the Kings Road, frees men to be individual in their dress, but Mods continue to favour a clean, crisp look. Designers such as Pierre Cardin, Ted Lapidus, Hardy Amies and John Weitz begin to dictate menswear trends. Films such as *Bonnie & Clyde* awaken a new interest in 1930s dressing. In France, the Renoma look, modelled above by pop singer Jacques Dutronc, is hugely influential. In Italy ready-to-wear suits begin to overtake handmade garments.

1970s   1980s

Big shoulders, wide lapels and flares, pronounced waists and fancy weaves produce widespread exuberance. Synthetic fibres are widely popular and, unusually, suits are often in strong colours. Giorgio Armani deconstructs suits to provide ease and comfort. German and Scandinavian makers perfect 'the engineered suit'. Licensing makes a fortune for designers such as Armani, Valentino and Yves St Laurent, whose Autumn/Winter 1974 suits are shown here. Glam rock, *Saturday Night Fever* disco suits and Tommy Nutter on Savile Row up the fashion stakes for tailoring. But films such as *The Godfather, Chinatown, The Great Gatsby*, and *The Sting* encourage nostalgia for the looks of the 1920s and 1930s.

A decade of excess is encapsulated by Michael Douglas' power-dressing suits for his role as Gordon Gekko in *Wall Street* from 1987. The 'athletic cut' creates an inverted V-shape on suits. Gianni Versace, Giorgio Armani and Hugo boss all benefit from the craze for *Miami Vice*-style casual or shiny suits (above). Versace is the Italian flashy riposte to Armani's usual restraint. In Paris, Jean Paul Gaultier's wide shoulders and tight body section distort the suit's usual proportions. Even 1930s zoot suits enjoy a limited revival thanks to Kid Creole. Suit sales sometimes benefit from the trend to dress up to socialise but in Silicon Valley and elsewhere dress-down casualwear undermines the suit's position.

1990s   2000s

In a decade that gives us grunge and lots of sportswear, suits take a relatively low profile. Simple black SB suits are everywhere. The austere high-fashion looks of Helmut Lang and Jil Sander are developed further by Prada and then by many imitators from the mainstream. Even on the big screen, Tarantino's *Reservoir Dogs* (1992) and *Pulp Fiction* (1994) and the sci-fi comedy *Men in Black* (1997) champion a monochrome, pared-down look. But the beginnings of a bespoke suit revival are spotted on Savile Row, where in 1992, Richard James (above) is the first of the new generation of British tailors to open up shop on the venerable street. Technical 'performance' fabrics become increasingly important.

The new millennium begins with renewed interest in luxury names, such as the Tom Ford-driven Gucci and later his YSL. The American then starts a fashion business under his own name. Hedi Slimane's superslim collections for Dior Homme launches dozens of imitators and re-interests younger consumers in fashion suits. The desire for personalised fashion leads to a notable revival in made-to-measure and Savile Row enjoys a strong renaissance. Even more than designers, the new style arbiters are celebrities from Hollywood, music, reality TV and sport, such as Christiano Ronaldo, here wearing a suit by Savile Row-based William Hunt as he picks up his FIFA World Player of the Year award in 2009.

Index

Endnotes

Chapter 1 *Convention or Fashion?*

1 Norah Waugh, *The Cut of Men's Clothes 1600–1900* (quoted by Hardy Amies, *The Englishman's Suit*, p. 11)
2 James Laver, quoted by Hardy Amies, Ibid., p. 12
3 James Laver, *Costume and Fashion: A Concise History*, p. 158
4 Norah Waugh, quoted by Hardy Amies, *The Englishman's Suit*, p. 13
5 Amies, Ibid., p. 11
6 Eric Sigsworth, *Montague Burton: The Tailor of Taste*, p. 59
7 Laver, *Costume and Fashion*, p. 260
8 Colin McDowell, *The Man of Fashion: Peacock Males and Perfect Gentlemen*, p. 119
9 Rodney Bennett-England, *Dress Optional*, pp. 60–1
10 O E Schoeffler and William Gale, *Esquire's Encyclopaedia of 20th-Century Men's Fashions*, p. 41
11 *Menswear*, August 2001, p. 12

Chapter 2 *A Question of Balance*

1 James Sherwood, *The London Cut: Savile Row Bespoke Tailoring*, p. 12
2 O E Schoeffler and William Gale, *Esquire's Encyclopaedia of 20th-Century Men's Fashions*, pp. 513–14
3 Hardy Amies, *The Englishman's Suit*, pp. 102–3
4 Amies, Ibid., p. 41
5 Nicholas Antongiavanni, *The Suit*, p. 19
6 Amies, *The Englishman's Suit*, p. 109

Chapter 3 *Princes Among Men*

1 Quoted by Edward, Duke of Windsor, *A Family Album*, p. 30
2 Ibid., p. 12
3 Ibid., pp. 13–14
4 Ibid., p. 35
5 Colin McDowell, *The Man of Fashion: Peacock Males and Perfect Gentlemen*, p. 86
6 A Gernsheim, quoted by Valerie Cumming, *Royal Dress: The Image and Reality, 1580 to the Present Day*, p. 148–9
7 *A Family Album*, p. 31
8 *Men's Wear*, 16 February 1952, p. 23
9 *A Family Album*, p. 35
10 Ibid., p. 1–3
11 Ibid., p. 105–6
12 Ibid., p. 114
13 Nicholas Antongiavanni, *The Suit*, p. 60

Chapter 4 *The Italian Job*

1 Farid Chenoune and Jay McInerney, *Brioni*, p. 13
2 Ibid., p. 13
3 Colin McDowell, *The Man of Fashion: Peacock Males and Perfect Gentlemen*, p. 138

Chapter 5 *US Male*

1 Nicholas Antongiavanni, *The Suit*, pp. 182–3

Chapter 6 *Passion From Paris*

1 Nik Cohn, *Today There Are No Gentlemen: The Changes in Englishmen's Clothes Since The War*, p. 75
2 Colin McDowell, *The Man of Fashion: Peacock Males and Perfect Gentlemen*, p. 145
3 Farid Chenoune, *A History of Men's Fashion*, pp. 276–7
4 Rodney Bennett-England, *Dress Optional: The Revolution in Menswear*, p. 95
5 Chenoune, *A History of Men's Fashion*, p. 276
6 Ibid., p. 263
7 Ibid., p. 267
8 McDowell, *The Man of Fashion: Peacock Males and Perfect Gentlemen*, p. 197

Chapter 7 *Lost in Music*

1 Stuart Jackson, *A Portrait of Duke Ellington, Reminiscing In Tempo*, p. 23
2 Paul Gorman, *The Look: Adventures in Rock and Pop Fashion*, p. 12
3 Interview included on *The Strange World of Northern Soul* (Wienerworld DVD, 2003)
4 Gorman, *The Look: Adventures in Rock and Pop Fashion*, p. 216

Chapter 8 *The Magic of the Movies*

1 Quoted by Deborah Nadoolman Landis in *Dressed: A Century Of Hollywood Costume Design*, p. 332

Bibliography

Amies, Hardy, *An ABC of Men's Fashion*, Newnes Key Book, 1964.

Amies, Hardy, *Still Here*, Weidenfeld and Nicolson, 1984.

Amies, Hardy, *The Englishman's Suit*, Quartet Books, 1994.

Antongiavanni, Nicholas, *The Suit: A Machiavellian Approach to Men's Style*, Collins, 2006.

Bennett-England, Rodney, *Dress Optional: The Revolution in Menswear*, Peter Owen, 1967.

Breward, Christopher, *Fashion*, Oxford University Press, 2003.

Breward, Christopher, *Fashioning London: Clothing and the Modern Metropolis*, Berg 2004.

Breward, Christopher, *The Hidden Consumer: Masculinities, Fashion and City Life 1860–1914*, Manchester University Press, 1999.

Breward, Christopher, Gilbert, David and Lister, Jenny, *Swinging Sixties: Fashion in London and beyond 1955–1970*, V&A Publications, 2006.

Breward, Christopher, Ehrman, Edwina and Evans, Caroline, *The London Look: Fashion from Street to Catwalk*, Yale University Press, 2004.

Byrde, Penelope, *The Male Image: Men's Fashion in Britain 1300–1970*, B T Batsford, 1979.

Chenoune, Farid, *A History of Men's Fashion*, Flammarion, 1993.

Chenoune, Farid, *Jean Paul Gaultier*, Assouline, 2005.

Chenoune, Farid and McInerney, Jay, *Brioni*, Universe/Vendome, 1998.

Cicolini, Alice, *The New English Dandy*, Thames & Hudson, 2005.

Cohn, Nik, *Today There Are No Gentlemen: The Changes in Englishmen's Clothes Since the War*, Weidenfeld and Nicolson, 1971.

Constantino, Maria, *Men's Fashion in the Twentieth Century: From Frock Coats to Intelligent Fibres*, B T Batsford, 1997.

Cooke, John William, *Generations of Style, It's All About the Clothes*, Brooks Brothers, 2003.

Cumming, Valerie, *Royal Dress: The Image and Reality, 1580 to the Present Day*, B T Batsford, 1989.

Dall'ara, Renzo, *Lubiam: Un Uomo, Una Storia*, Editorale Sometti, 1999.

Edward, Duke of Windsor, *A Family Album*, Cassell, 1960.

Flusser, Alan, *Dressing the Man: Mastering the Art of Permanent Fashion*, Harper Collins, 2002.

Gavenas, Mary Lisa, *The Fairchild Encyclopaedia of Menswear*, Fairchild Publications, 2008.

Giorgetti, Cristina and others, *Brioni: Fifty Years of Style*, Octavo, 1995.

Gorman, Paul, *The Look: Adventures in Rock and Pop Fashion*, Adelita, 2006.

Hardy, Phil (ed.), *The Overlook Film Encyclopaedia: The Gangster Film*, Overlook, 1998.

Howarth, Stephen, *Henry Poole, Founders of Savile Row: The Making of a Legend*, Bene Factum Publishing, 2003.

Jackson, Stuart, *A Portrait of Duke Ellington, Reminiscing In Tempo*, Sidgwick & Jackson, 1999.

Landis, Deborah Nadoolman, *Dressed: A Century of Hollywood Costume Design*, Collins Design, 2007.

Laver, James, *Clothes*, Burke, 1952.

Laver, James, *Costume and Fashion: A Concise History*, Thames & Hudson, 2002.

Lorin, Philippe and Oudin, Sara, *Dormeuil: The history of fabric is woven into the fabric of history*, Dormeuil Frères, 1992.

Lurie, Alison, *The Language of Clothes*, Heinemann, 1981.

Maneker, Marion, *Dressing in the Dark: Lessons in Men's Style from the Movies*, Assouline, 2002.

McDowell, Colin, *Dressed to Kill: Sex, Power & Clothes*, Hutchinson, 1992.

McDowell, Colin, *Fashion Today*, Phaidon Press, 2000.

McDowell, Colin, *The Man of Fashion: Peacock Males and Perfect Gentlemen*, Thames & Hudson, 1997.

McDowell, Colin (ed.), *The Pimlico Companion to Fashion*, Pimlico, 1998.

Middlemas, Keith, *The Life and Times of Edward VII*, Weidenfeld and Nicolson, 1972.

O'Hara, Georgina Callan, *Dictionary of Fashion and Fashion Designers*, Thames & Hudson, 1998.

Schoeffler, O E and Gale, William, *Esquire's Encyclopaedia of 20th Century Men's Fashions*, McGraw-Hill, 1973.

Sigsworth, Eric, *Montague Burton: The Tailor of Taste*, Manchester University Press, 1990.

Sherwood, James, *The London Cut: Savile Row Bespoke Tailoring*, Marsilio, 2007.

Walker, Richard, *The Savile Row Story: An Illustrated History*, Prion, 1988.

Watt, Judith (ed.), *The Penguin Book of Twentieth-Century Fashion Writing*, Viking, 1999.

Wayne, Jane Ellen, *The Leading Men of MGM*, Carroll & Graf, 2005.

Woodhead, Colin and others, *Dressed to Kill: James Bond, the Suited Hero*, Flammarion, 1996.

Ziegler, Philip, *King Edward VIII: The Official Biography*, Collins, 1990.

Magazines

Sir: Men's International Fashion Journal, 1955–86

Men's Wear, 1902–2002

Acknowledgements

I would like to acknowledge the many people who have knowingly or unknowingly educated me on suits during the nearly thirty years I have been writing about the fashion business. For specifically assisting with this book I would like to express my gratitude to Diane Almond, Katharine Baird, David Belcher, Yves Benbaste, Simon Berwin, Malcolm Bird, Nöelle Bobin, Tom Bottomley, Klaus Brinkmann, Simon Carter, Gino Da'Prato, Antonella de Simone, Jane Eastoe, Timothy Everest, Beverley Forrest, David Harvey, Douglas Hood, Olivier Lapidus, Günter Leibold, Stephen Mahoney, Khabi Mirza, Ian Moon, Chris Moore, Greta Pawlowski, Carlo Rivetti, Thomas Rasch, Phil Shaw, Manny Silverman, Philip Start, Kevin Stone, Frank Smith, Stanley Tucker, Richard Vaughan-Davies and Colin Woodhead for their time, memories, assistance, photos and books. My thanks also go to Emma O'Neill for her indefatigable picture research, to Georgina Hewitt for her enthusiasm as my designer at Pavilion Books, to Emily Preece-Morrison for guiding the project at Pavilion Books, and to Polly Powell at Anova Books for the original idea and the commission.

Eric Musgrave

The publishers would like to thank the following individuals and organisations for supplying images for this book.

Cover images:
Front: **Woolmark Archive (Australian Wool Innovation Ltd.) and London College of Fashion.**
Back: **Rex Features/Everett Collection.**
Endpapers: **From the Brioni Archive.**

Images courtesy of The Advertising Archives 25, 41, 88–89; **akg-images** 188, /Album/A/Karen Ballard/M.G.M 172; **Courtesy the Aquascutum Archives** 45; **From the Brioni Archive** 38, 81; **Camera Press/Eyedea** 119, /BOTTI/STILLS 55 left, 122–123; **Catwalking.com** 54 right, 69 right, 70 left, 91, 129 bottom; **Corbis** 115 left, /Paul Adelman 112–113, /Jeff Albertson 156, /Bettmann 42, 70-71, 103, 107, 108, 150–151, 190 right, /Bureau L.A. Collection/Sygma 167, /Frank Carroll/Sygma 29, /Elisabetta Catalano/Condé Nast Archive 87, /Cat's Collection 2, /CinemaPhoto 109, /Pierre Fournier/Sygma 145, /Hulton-Deutsch Collection 52-53, /Robbie Jack 146, /LE SEGRETAIN PASCAL/ Sygma 101, /Patrick Lichfield/Condé Nast Archive 4, /Michael Ochs Archives 95, /Norman Parkinson Limited 10, /Sunset Boulevard/Sygma 168-169; **Dormeuil Archives** 127, 133, 135, /Chale 134, /René Gruau 132; **For Him Magazine** /Tim Blake 83; **Getty Images** /Alan Band/Hulton Archive 110, /Central Press/ Hulton Archive 190 left, /Fin Costello/Redferns 158-159, /W & D Downey/Hulton Archive 63, /Alfred Eisenstaedt/Time & Life Pictures 72 left, /Evening Standard 72 right, /Fotos International/Hulton Archive 55 right, /GAB Archives/Redferns 148, /Ross Gilmore/ Redferns 157, /Tim Graham/Hulton Archive 192 left, /Hulton Archive 13, 16, 22, 27, 189 right, /Kurt Hutton/Hulton Archive 15, /Jones/Hulton Archive 46, /Keystone/Hulton Archive 64, 114 left, /Reg Lancaster/Hulton Archive 128, /Lipnitzki/Roger Viollet 75, 117, /London Stereoscopic Company/Hulton Archive 114 right, /Mansell/Time & Life Pictures 59, /Michael Ochs Archives 47, 138, 154, 162 left, 191 left, /Douglas Miller/Hulton Archive 48, /Terry O'Neill 153, 163, /Silver Screen Collection/Hulton Archive 51, /Chip Somodevilla 102, /Terrence Spencer/Time & Life Pictures 30-31, /Christopher Simon Sykes/Hulton Archive 73 left, /Gai Terrell/Redferns 141, /Tim Graham Photo Library 66, 67, /Richard Upper/Redferns 93 right, /David Warner – Ellis Photography/ Redferns 137, /Robert Whitaker/Hulton Archive 11; **Hickey Freeman Circa 1968** 92 right; **INTERFOTO** /Schultheiss 86; **The Isaia Archive** 79; **Richard James, photograph by John Spinks** 7, 193 left; **The Kobal Collection** 106, 177; **Courtesy of The Lapidus Family** 130; **Magnum** /Richard Kalvar 129 top; **Mary Evans Picture Library** 17, 19, 189 left, /MARY EVANS – ILN PICTURES 68-69; **Mirrorpix** 33 right, 104-105; **Offside** /L'Equipe 193 right; **Photofest** 115 right, 173, 183; **Photos12.com** /Collection Cinéma 90; **JL Rancurel/Rancurel Phototèque** 191 right; **Rex Features** /20C.Fox/Everett Collection 181, /Everett Collection 28, 54 left, 98, 165, 170, 175, 176, 178–179, 180, 185, 186-187, /Dezo Hoffmann 49, 152, /ITV 61, /NBCUPHOTOBANK 192 right, /C.Tavin/Everett Collection 57, 182, /Richard Young 160; **Photo copyright Mick Rock 1973, 2009** 162 right; **Chuck Stewart** 149; **TOM FORD BY SOLVE SUNDSBO** 85; **TopFoto** /Ken Russell 26; **V&A Images** /Harry Hammond 142-143; **Picture by Bruce Weber, 1998, courtesy of Polo Ralph Lauren** 111; **Woolmark Archive (Australian Wool Innovation Ltd.) and London College of Fashion** 9, 32 left & right, 33 left, 35, 73 right, 82, 92 left, 93 left, 131.

We apologise in advance for any unintentional omission or neglect and will be pleased to insert the appropriate acknowledgment for any companies or individuals in any subsequent edition of this work.

For my wife Jane, who always loves to see me in a suit, and for my mother Louisa, who got used to my wardrobe excesses years ago.

First published in the United Kingdom in 2009 by
PAVILION BOOKS
10 Southcombe Street, London, W14 0RA

An imprint of Anova Books Company Ltd

Design and layout © Pavilion, 2009
Text © Eric Musgrave, 2009
Photography © see acknowledgements on page 199

Senior editor: Emily Preece-Morrison
Designer: Georgina Hewitt
Picture researcher: Emma O'Neill
Copy editor: Ian Allen
Proofreader: Naomi Waters
Indexer: Patricia Hymans
Production: Rebekah Cheyne

ISBN 978–1–86205–852–1

A CIP catalogue record for this book is available
from the British Library.

10 9 8 7 6 5 4 3 2 1

Reproduction by Dot Gradations Ltd, UK
Printed and bound by 1010 Printing International Ltd, China

www.anovabooks.com